COSMO COOKERY

GOURMET MEALS FROM THE
FIRST DRINK TO THE LAST KISS

COSMOPOLITAN BOOKS

ACKNOWLEDGMENTS

Many COSMOPOLITAN editors, writers, readers—plus their
lovers, husbands, and friends—contributed ideas and recipes
to this book, tasted and reported on the menus, and earned
our gratitude and affection. And one rather special person,
Margot Higgins—international food and nutrition expert—
translated our cleverness into intelligent practicality.
Her kitchen expertise is the source behind the meticulous
instructions for making everything in this book. Truly,
potential disasters were transformed into succulent successes
through her guidance. Bless you, Margot!

COSMOPOLITAN BOOKS
Editorial Director Helen Gurley Brown
Editor-in-Chief Jeanette Sarkisian Wagner
Assistant Editor Veronica Geng
Copy Editor Ellen Tabak
Editorial Assistant Tiena-Kay Halm

CONTENTS:

FOREWORD
Helen Gurley Brown
page vii

HOW TO USE THIS BOOK
page ix

CHAPTER 1
YOUR KITCHEN
AND WHAT TO PUT IN IT
page 1

CHAPTER 2
EVERYTHING
MOTHER HUBBARD WISHED SHE'D
HAD IN HER CUPBOARD
page 9

CHAPTER 3
SETTING THE SCENE
page 17

CHAPTER 4
DINNER MENUS
page 25

CHAPTER 5
BRUNCH MENUS
page 163

CHAPTER 6
SEDUCTIVE SWEETS
page 199

CHAPTER 7
SENSE-REELING DRINKS
page 211

CHAPTER 8
FINGER FOODS
page 221

AFTERWORD
Jeanette Sarkisian Wagner
page 237

INDEX
page 242

FOREWORD

You've just refilled his glass with that exquisite Montrachet, and together you lie in bed, nibbling a Cognac-laced pâté. . . . Doesn't a sensuous *mood* steal over you both, suggesting the soft, enveloping, passionate love-union to follow? And after sexual energy is spent, perhaps you prolong your mutual pleasure by sharing a delicious meal!

There *is* a relationship between food and sex. You might say the connection is *symbiotic,* because one appetite can *feed* the other in a never-ending cycle of sensation. In both, we *need* sustenance, but *crave* enjoyment, too.

The Romans understood these links between one delight and another. They reveled in the *sensuality* of a meal: elaborately decorated, succulent gourmet foods, mouth-caressing sauces, dining rooms heady with rare scents and softened with voluptuous cushions, pleasant entertainments for eye and ear . . . spending hours to *savor* every morsel, making food the transition to further tempting delectations. Why, even those maligned *Victorians* produced chefs of genius and took an almost *lustful* joy in leisurely, luscious banquets (maybe to make up for *sexual* deprivation!)

Well, where have *we* come from those periods? Not very far—we've practically *regressed!* Electronic expertise, thank you, gives us the con-temporary kitchen, but how do many people *use* this miracle? For speedy meals, that's how! . . . something defrosted and cooked in twenty, gobbled in ten unaware minutes. As the French (so *wise* about food-for-pleasure) would say, *quel* waste!

Some people (and since you're reading this, you're probably one of them) instinctively know that food is *more* than merely life-maintaining. I think you would agree with a little-known California cook *supreme,* who says, "Cooking must at all times be fun, sexy, and liberated." That's what *Cosmo Cookery* is all about . . . learning how to use food for *total* enjoyment (that means *you* enjoy as well as your man or any guests). And in this book you're now reading, COSMO's experts detail every step.

First, we'll find out how to organize even the tiniest speck of a kitchen into a *model* of efficiency, stocked with the utensils and staple foods you'll *really* need at hand. Next, learn our crafty techniques for creating *atmosphere,* to make eating an appeal to eye, ear, smell, touch, as *well* as taste. Now you're ready for our forty-six elegant dinner menus (yes, I expect you to use *all* of them!) planned from the first drink until that last kiss (which you'll surely *deserve* for being such a marvelous culinary temptress!) Specific instructions tell how to prepare and serve *every* item on *every* menu, right down to accompanying wines, desserts, liqueurs. Should someone happen to stay on . . . and on . . . turn to the brunch chapter and choose from the dozen mouth-watering menus for those lazy days when everyone wants to rise late and be *pampered*. (*Try* pampering cuisine-style and see what dividends you reap!)

The final chapters of *Cosmo Cookery* round up super recipes to supplement your now-growing repertoire of desserts and beverages (from exotic coffees to libations sure to please even the most *discriminating* wine-and-spirits fancier).

In creating this book, we've built in as much infallibility as possible. *Any* cook can make a mistake, even the most experienced, but we've tried to eliminate all but your own human error. (Yes, you *could* be making love while the quiche blackens in the oven . . . that's *your* decision!) The recipes are uncomplicated, but they couldn't bore even the most *jaded* palate. By following instructions and using the superb ingredients recommended, you'll achieve success every time, accompanied by a *deserved* reputation for gourmet skill. Remember, you needn't be encyclopedic about cooking to win appreciation. Doing a *few* delicious taste-gratifiers *very well* creates an over-all effect that guests will never forget.

Follow the advice of Gael Greene, a Cosmopolitan writer and New York food critic: "A woman does well to be beautiful, mysterious, haunting, witty, rich, and exotic in bed . . . but it never hurts to cook good." *Cosmo Cookery* should take care of the latter. Enjoy!

Helen Gurley Brown
EDITOR-IN-CHIEF, COSMOPOLITAN

HOW TO USE THIS BOOK

We've simply *packed* every chapter with information—factual and creative—and we want to help you make the *most* of it *all*. So please do read Chapters 1, 2, and 3 *before* selecting one of our meticulously planned dinner or brunch menus for your next special feast.

After glancing over our guidelines, determine what basic equipment *you* have to work with. Then simply go through all the menus until you find one *you* like best. First, study the *entire* meal plan, from supply list to preparing and serving the meal, *before* writing your marketing list. Be sure you understand everything you're going to do, and that you have the necessary equipment (or good substitutes) to complete the menu. This step-by-step approach saves so much *later* grief. (Don't you *hate* to get to the "Serve the dessert . . . " paragraph only to discover, *alas too late,* that you need lemon peels for the espresso?)

The *Cosmo Cookery* menus are especially planned so that all the elements complement each other. Of course, you *may* make substitutes . . . from your own favorites to recipes listed elsewhere in this book. If you do that, try to *match* flavors to keep the meal balanced: That is, if you want to replace a suggested green vegetable, don't substitute a *starch* . . . use another green vegetable. If you don't want a mandarin orange salad, substitute a similar fruit-and-green salad . . . *not* cole slaw.

Take note here also of the abbreviations we'll be using throughout the book:

tsp. = teaspoon
tbsp. = tablespoon
c. = cup
oz. = ounce
lb. = pound
pt. = pint

These are all for *standard* measures, so do make sure to use standard measuring spoons and cups when following recipes.

Enjoy *all* your adventures abetted by this book. And good eating—in eleven languages!

Bon appetit!
Buon appetito!
Guten appetit!
Buen apetito!
God aptit!
God appetit!
B'tay a'von!
Priytnago appetita!
Tanoshinde tabete kudasai!
Kaì wei shih chen!
Hearty appetite!

CHAPTER 1

YOUR
KITCHEN
AND WHAT
TO PUT IN IT

Ah, yes, it *would* be nice to have a combination country kitchen and living room, complete with fireplace and brick walls. After all, it *is* a nuisance to be bending languidly over the stove, out of sight, when you would *prefer* to bend sensuously over a handsome guest. But until you reach an economic level where you can hire an architect to build a kitchen to suit *you, hang* the cost, you'll probably have to cope with cooking space that is really smaller than you'd like and away from guests. Don't despair. *Convenience* is what really counts, and *with planning* your kitchen will *work.*

The first two things to think about (before you unpack or buy anything!) are storage and working space: You need cupboards or shelves to store groceries, cooking equipment, appliances, and tools. A basic rule: If you really *use* all your equipment, keep it *easily* available. That super-duper ten-speed electric blender stored in its packing box at the top of a six-foot shelf is not handy, so you *won't* use it. If, however, there are some dishes and cooking pots only used when entertaining *large* numbers, put those in the *least* accessible places. Simply remember to take them out and clean them a day before the party.

It may be best, if kitchen storage is *very* limited, to keep china, crystal, silver, in a chest in the dining or living area. Steps are saved when setting the table, and these items stay cleaner away from cooking smells and grease.

Don't, repeat *don't,* occupy limited counter space with appliances needed once a month (or not at all), or with ornamental canisters and casseroles, unless used daily. Allow elbow room to chop onions, parsley, green pepper, someplace to set out plates on which you will serve the meal, an area to stack dishes and glasses after dinner.

These are a few tricks some girls have developed to maximize space: If there's room, tuck in a tiny *extra* work table. Or if you have a gap between where your counter ends and the stove (or sink) begins, extend the counter by installing a wooden chopping block between counter and stove, one end resting on each. Or build in a fold-down shelf on a wall area where nothing else must be hung.

In fact, bare walls may turn out to be the best storage space of all. A pegboard is wonderful for hanging most pots, pans, large work utensils (beaters, whisks, slotted spoons, meat forks, etc.) Paint the pegboard a gay color, making outlines of every pan/pot if you wish to show where each should be put. Magnetic strips screwed to the wall accommodate knives and keep them from dulling (what happens when they're cluttered together in a drawer). Simple wooden spice racks can be fixed on the wall, or suspended below cabinets; don't store spices near the stove—heat and moisture deteriorate their flavor.

Check hardware and department stores for ingenious racks and dividers that can be installed in cabinets to double available space. Plastic dividers in kitchen drawers make small tools much easier to find: Put all wooden implements in one area, whisks, choppers, and peelers in another, corkscrew and bottle openers elsewhere. You should be able to find any utensil with your eyes shut: Strict order is the professional way to store equipment, and good for self-confidence.

Extend the usefulness of cabinet space by installing a narrow raised shelf at the back of cupboards. You won't knock over items in the front row while reaching for something behind them, and the storage space doubles.

1 VISIBILITY IS IMPORTANT

Make sure lighting in the kitchen is *excellent*. Use powerful bulbs if outlets are limited; install a fluorescent fixture or hanging light over the main work area. This is not the room for romantic candleglow—if that's what you now have, then cooking dinner will, literally, give you a headache.

2 APPLIANCES

When buying electric appliances, shop for quality. Name brands, even if a trifle more expensive, give long and reliable service and can be repaired, usually locally, if necessary. It's a good idea to compare brands before buying: Consult the annual *Consumer Reports* buying guide, *Facts You Need Before You Buy* (available from *Consumer Reports,* 256 Washington Street, Mount Vernon, New York, 10550; $2.65).

A toaster and percolator (or whatever kind of coffee maker you prefer) are *important* investments: Buy good ones and *large* ones. The coffee maker should hold twelve cups; the toaster should have wide openings—in addition to toasting bread, you may want to use it for muffins and coffee cake. We prefer horizontal toasters for that reason; all sizes of breads fit.

A small electric beater (not necessarily the kind with a stand and various bowls) is a useful ally, super for whipping cream, egg whites, and cake batter without muscle collapse. And a blender is a *joy* . . . not *essential* to survival but worth every penny of the thirty dollars or so it costs. Creaming soups, frosting daiquiris, and making fine bread crumbs are only a few of the functions it performs.

After you acquire these four basic appliances, consider carefully how much storage space can be spared for other additions. A hot tray is useful if you plan to entertain often; a sandwich-waffle grill is fun; an electric skillet is excellent for long, slow cooking jobs such as stews, baked beans, as well as just frying. If you would enjoy and use these appliances often, then they'll earn their space; if not, avoid the expense. Electric can openers, knife sharpeners, and other gadgets are splendid, especially if someone happens to give them to you as a house gift. In the meantime, dime-store versions are adequate.

There's at least one nonelectric appliance that is mandatory for cachet in the kitchen—an espresso pot to make superb after-dinner coffee. In addition, a cocktail shaker is essential, since many drinks need shaking, not merely stirring. We recommend the standard chrome model that professional bartenders use: It's cheaper and more durable than luxurious ones of silver and crystal.

3 POTS AND PANS

Buy quality. Thin, cheap pans won't do a good job and don't last. Choose heavy aluminum, enameled cast iron, or stainless steel. Clean these properly and they'll last your lifetime. Food prepared in such pans cooks steadily and *evenly,* without burning or scorching.

Before buying, do some comparative shopping. If your city has a restaurant supply house (try the Yellow Pages for leads) drop in and look at what's available. Talk to the proprietor . . . tell him you're a beginning cook, or one who loves to cook but doesn't know too much about hardware. Listen to his advice; compare prices with the best housewares department in town.

Don't buy tiny frying pans or small sauté pans. You can always cook for one person in a large pan, but small pans have very limited uses.

Heavy copper is wonderful, of course, but has many disadvantages for an amateur cook. For one thing it's frightfully expensive. Then it needs polishing after *every* use. Copper must be lined, usually with tin; and when this lining wears, it must be replated, a service not always easy to find and not necessarily cheap.

Don't buy more than you need. For the average small kitchen three or four saucepans and two or three frying/sauté pans are enough (all need covers). See specific list at the end of this chapter.

4 CASSEROLES AND BAKING DISHES

Any housewares department offers a dazzling array of every color and shape of casserole. Don't be mesmerized by the patterns. The most practical are enameled cast iron . . . more durable and versatile than pottery, glass, or china, as it can be used over a flame as well as in the oven.

Recommended: oval casseroles instead of round ones . . . seem to take different-shaped meats and vegetables more easily. Buy them with lids. A set of Pyrex casseroles in various sizes is excellent for food you want to take right from the oven and store in the freezer for later use. Pyrex casseroles are specially treated to withstand extremes of temperature.

For baking, dime-store pie, muffin, and loaf tins, baking sheets, are excellent.

5 UTENSILS: KNIVES, FORKS, SPOONS, AND ASSORTED SMALL IMPLEMENTS

A collection of sharp knives is an important asset for any good cook. Don't economize here . . . you'll only make the work harder. Peeling, slicing, and chopping are so much easier with a first-class knife. The best French or German ones are carbon steel, not stainless, and for a good reason: They can be resharpened quickly and hold an edge much longer. Don't immerse them in water: Wipe with a damp cloth or sponge, dry after *every* use so they won't rust. Keep them on a rack, not thrown in a drawer. Sharpen them occasionally on a carborun-dum sharpening stone or on a butcher's steel—both available in good kitchen-supply departments. (Note: If you buy an electric can opener, choose one that has a knife-sharpening opening . . . it's marvelous!)

Buy a sturdy, heavy chopping board made of a solid block of wood (pieced boards warp, have cracks difficult to clean food out of) not less than a foot square. One variety comes with a removable plastic bowl into which you push chopped items as they are done, thus keeping the board clear; the handy bowl makes it easy to transfer chopped items to the pan. Do not soak any wood utensils or boards in water . . . that warps them. Wash quickly, dry immediately.

6 MISCELLANEOUS NEEDS

The balance of your *batterie de cuisine* (what French chefs call their essential tools) need not be expensive. However, if you buy a rotary eggbeater, buy a good one . . . the cheap variety is nearly useless. Actually, if you have a few whisks (see list at end of chapter) and an electric beater, you won't need a rotary beater at all.

You'll need a few mixing bowls, sturdy plastic containers for storing leftovers, two or three serving dishes and platters.

Mixing bowls of pottery or glass are better than plastic, which retains odors and often is too light for beating purposes. Stainless steel is excellent, but a bit extravagant. A copper bowl is even *more* extravagant, but French cooks recommend for beating egg whites. (For chemical reasons, they fluff faster in copper.)

For salads, fruit platters, cheese and crackers, we recommend plain glass plates . . . also good as service plates for ice cream and custard dishes.

One last word before checking out of the kitchen. Dishwashing is a bore, but doing it efficiently lightens the load and adds to the life expectancy of your treasures. At the dime store buy a colored plastic dishpan, matching drainer. Collect attractive printed linen dish towels for drying crystal (leave no lint), choose terry cloth ones (no ironing!) for pots and pans. Use scalding hot water for washing (wear rubber gloves to protect your hands and nails), and rinse everything in the hottest water possible. Don't put dirty dishes in the sink or in the pan—that's how most chips and cracks happen. Stack them to the right of your sink, do one piece at a time. (Note: If you rinse food off plates immediately after removing from the table and stack them carefully, you can ignore the pile until guests leave. Then the washing chore will be very quick. Coagulated food is not only ugly, but hard to remove.) When everything is thoroughly dry (next day), put it away gently. If you're not in total collapse, polish off any stains on silver or silver plate before you store it. How disconcerting to set the table just before a party and find silver forks discolored from the omelet you served a week ago! If you keep copper and silver polish next to your regular cleaner, you'll discipline yourself.

YOUR BASIC EQUIPMENT LIST

SPACE SAVERS AND ORGANIZERS
Knife rack
Pegboard or pot rack
Cupboard dividers or storage trays
Stacking shelves
Spice rack
Knife trays for small implements
Cup rack

2. ELECTRIC AND OTHER APPLIANCES
Toaster
Percolator or other coffee maker
Electric or hand beater
Blender
Espresso coffee pot
Cocktail shaker and strainer
Pitcher for stirring martinis, iced tea, or coffee
Sandwich-waffle grill (optional)
Hot tray (optional)
Electric skillet (optional)

3. POTS AND PANS
3 heavy saucepans, assorted sizes, for instance: $1\frac{1}{2}$ quart, $2\frac{1}{2}$ quart, 4 quart
1 large saucepan for spaghetti, etc., about 10-quart size
1 large, heavy skillet with lid, about 12" across
1 medium skillet, about 9" across
1 small skillet, 6" or 7" across
1 medium omelet pan with slanted sides, 7" across bottom (optional)
1 roasting pan with cover
1 large colander for straining spaghetti or vegetables
double boiler
chafing dish, or fondue pot and heater (optional)
griddle (optional)
teakettle (optional)

4. CASSEROLES AND BAKING DISHES
1 deep casserole with lid, 6-quart or larger

1 set smaller casseroles
1 or 2 shallow baking dishes
6 or more individual casseroles (cocottes)
1 or 2 pie tins (optional)
1 or 2 baking sheets (optional)
muffin pan (optional)
loaf pan (optional)

5. KNIVES, FORKS, SPOONS, AND SMALL IMPLEMENTS
1 large chopping knife
2 or 3 smaller knives for paring and slicing
1 bread knife with serrated edge
1 grapefruit knife
1 long, thin knife for carving or slicing
knife-sharpening steel or carborundum stone (optional)
1 large 2-pronged kitchen fork
2 or 3 regular kitchen forks
4 wooden spoons
1 large basting spoon
1 slotted or perforated spoon
1 set measuring spoons
liquid-measuring cup, 1-cup or 1-pint size; these have some space between top measuring-line and top of cup so liquids won't spill over
1 set solid-measuring cups; these come in plastic, and you fill to the top with flour, etc., and level with a knife to get exact amounts
1 ladle for soup, etc.

Other Tools
tongs
1 small wire whisk
1 medium wire whisk
1 spatula
1 pancake turner
1 small strainer
1 vegetable peeler
1 lemon squeezer
1 garlic press (optional)
1 pepper mill

1 corkscrew

1 bottle opener

1 nutcracker

1 meat tenderizer (like a hammer)

1 grater

1 rubber scraper

1 can opener

1 pastry brush

1 set small skewers

1 set large skewers for shish kebab (optional)

1 ice crusher (optional)

6. MISCELLANEOUS

3 or 4 mixing bowls, various sizes

1 heavy chopping board

2 or 3, or more, platters, dishes, and bowls for serving

1 good-sized wooden salad bowl

6 or more individual salad plates

1 oven thermometer, as a check on the oven thermostat

1 asbestos simmering pad, to reduce heat under pans
        when necessary

2 or 3 serving trays, large and small

1 timer

3 or 4 glass or plastic canisters for flour, sugar, etc.

CHAPTER 2

EVERYTHING
MOTHER HUBBARD
WISHED
SHE'D HAD
IN HER
CUPBOARD

It's *totally* demoralizing to discover you can't whip up your special spaghetti alla carbonara for that unexpected (but very welcome) visitor because you don't have any bacon or Parmesan cheese in the larder. Listen, smart girl, you must *always* keep staples, seasonings, and spices on hand. Replenish them *before* they run out . . . especially ingredients for your favorite recipes.

Here are our basic-supply suggestions, divided into groups. In each the obvious necessities come first, followed by items you may not want to keep on hand if storage space is limited, but which you may want because they are required for some recipes in this book.

1. GRAINS AND BREADS

Flour (all-purpose)
Cornstarch
Rice
Spaghetti
Noodles
Oatmeal

Breakfast cereal
Pancake mix
Bread crumbs
Bread
Crackers (assorted)
Cookies

2. SWEETENINGS

Sugar:
   fine granulated
   brown
   cubes
Pancake syrup

Honey
Jam or jelly
Marmalade

3. SAUCES, DRESSINGS

Tomato ketchup
Worcestershire sauce
Tabasco or similar pepper-sauce
Soy sauce
Mustard (Dijon variety)
Oil, olive
Oil, cooking
Vinegar, white wine

Vinegar, red wine
Salad dressing (*make your own vinegar-and-oil the day it's served; keep bottled green goddess and Russian on hand; check bottle labels for brands with purest ingredients*)
Mayonnaise

4. BEVERAGES

Coffee (percolator or drip grind)
Coffee, espresso
Coffee, instant

Tea (never bags!)
Cocoa or chocolate

5. SEASONINGS AND SPICES

Salt (iodized)
Pepper:
   whole black
   ground white
   paprika
   cayenne

MOSTLY FOR SALADS
AND VEGETABLES
Basil
Caraway
Celery salt
Dill
Mint

MOSTLY FOR SAUCES,
STEWS, MEATS, SOUPS
Bay leaves
Chili powder
Oregano
Rosemary
Sage

Tarragon
MOSTLY FOR DESSERTS
Allspice
Cinnamon (ground and whole)
Cloves
Ginger
Nutmeg
FOR CURRY SAUCES
Cardamom seeds
Coriander seeds
Cumin seeds
Turmeric
Curry powder
MOSTLY FOR MEAT
Mustard, dry
Horseradish
Garlic powder

6. PERISHABLES

(to be stored in refrigerator; don't buy for more than a few days ahead, a week at most)

(a) Milk
   Cream
   Butter
   Cheese
   Eggs
   Bacon (optional)
(b) Lemons
   Limes
   Fresh fruit

Carrots
Celery
Onions
Potatoes
Salad greens
Tomatoes
Cucumber
Parsley
Garlic

In a kitchen that is light, cool, and airy, you don't have to keep potatoes and onions under refrigeration; but if your dear little kitchen is hot, damp, or dark, they'll deteriorate quickly (potatoes will sprout and onions go mushy . . . especially if kept together). Store vegetables separately, and do put them in fridge if it seems necessary.

It's also a good idea to keep a few canned things in stock if you have enough space (perhaps a top shelf). We suggest:

SOUP	VEGETABLES	FRUIT
Consommé	Tomatoes	Pineapple (crushed and chunks in natural juice)
Chicken broth	Tomato sauce	Peach halves
Beef bouillon	Tomato paste	Cherries
Clam chowder	Baby beets	Pear halves
Black bean	Small whole potatoes	
Cream of mushroom	Asparagus	
	Tiny peas	
	Kernel corn	

If you have a separate freezer, there's no problem about keeping meats, vegetables, and fruit juices always in stock. With only a *small* freezing compartment in the refrigerator, you'll need to select more carefully. We suggest: one pack each of three of your favorite vegetables (but use fresh ones whenever you can!), at least four cans of frozen orange juice, two of lemonade, limeade, or pineapple juice. Bread, cake, and sweet rolls *also* stay fresh in the freezing compartment. Keep two kinds of ice cream and one sherbet if you have room and if your freezer temperature reaches zero degrees or lower. (Otherwise ice cream gets soft.)

A few paper and "household" staples you'll need in the kitchen: plastic wrap, aluminum foil, paper towels, dishwashing powder (or liquid), scouring powder (or pads), various polishes for silver, copper, furniture. Add to these toothpicks, paper napkins (a nice big size), paper cups, straws, and light bulbs.

THE BAR:

What you keep on hand depends on many variables: whether you and your friends enjoy cocktails and wine or prefer beer, soft drinks; how much space you have for your "cellar"; how much money you feel like investing. Stocking a bar can be an expensive hobby!

We can't really tell you whether you should buy premium liquor or the "house brand" at your liquor store, because you and your friends are not like anybody else so far as taste is concerned. Some people recognize, appreciate, and insist on the best quality. Others don't know or care! *Some*, unfortunately, can't tell the difference in taste but are impressed by labels. (The latter order name-brands in a bar, frequently to sound sophisticated, but probably wouldn't really notice if somebody switched brands on them.)

However, bar-stocking isn't a contest. You want to please guests, whether they are connoisseurs or novices in the matter of wine and liquor, and so you'll steer a middle course. Select a good liquor store where the range of wine indicates knowledge and taste. It's usually best to buy a good California wine rather than an unknown French or

German one from the bargain bin. Do ask the sales clerk for advice: He'll probably be flattered and eager to help. If he tries to sell you a vintage Burgundy to go with pizza, *avanti* to another store!

Basic liquor requirements to make the drinks listed in our menus are:

1. SPIRITS

Dry gin, domestic or imported (English)

Scotch whiskey

Vodka

Blended or bourbon whiskey

Rum (Puerto Rican or Virgin Island)

Brandy (Cognac, Armagnac, or domestic)

2. APERITIF WINES AND DRINK INGREDIENTS

Sherry

Ginger wine (Stone's or Crabbie's for Whiskey Mac)

Vermouth, French (dry)

Vermouth, Italian (sweet)

Vermouth, flavored (e.g., Dubonnet, Positano, Carpano, Chambéry, etc.)

3. ASSORTED FLAVORINGS

Grenadine

Rose's lime juice

Angostura bitters

Orange bitters

Orange flower water

4. LIQUEURS

There are dozens of these, and selection is a matter for individual preference and money! The following are among the most popular, and may be used not only as after-dinner drinks, but sprinkled over ice cream or fresh fruit, and as an ingredient in certain cocktails.

Cointreau

Grand Marnier

Drambuie

Cassis

Triple Sec

Crème de menthe

Kahlúa

Crème de cacao

Kirsch

These are also sometimes offered as after-dinner drinks: brandy, port, Marsala, and Madeira. (The last three are sweet, in varying degrees.)

5. SOFT DRINKS AND MIXERS

Club soda

Ginger ale

Tonic (quinine water)

Coca-Cola, 7Up, or other favorites

Low-calorie mixers if desired

6. WINE

It's nice to have a few bottles of wine in reserve, and a small wine rack takes little space. Usually it's best to keep bottles on their sides, in as dark and cool a place as possible. When you use the wines recommended in the dinner menus, make a note of any you especially like, so you can buy an extra bottle for your "cellar." Most young collectors prefer to diversify rather than buy several of one kind: We suggest a red Burgundy for steak and other red meats; a red Chianti or Soave for spaghetti and Italian dishes; a Moselle, Rhine, or white Burgundy for fish, creamed chicken; and maybe some rosé for veal or fried chicken. You'll find out as you go along which are your favorites, and probably guests will thoughtfully add an occasional gift bottle to your growing collection.

CHAPTER **3**

A marvelous bonus about being invited *to* a party is the incentive to try a new makeup, wear the latest fashion-find, do something different with your hair, add a bit of wild jewelry, an exotic scent.

When *you* hostess the party, the same concept should apply to your apartment. Giving a lift to your all-too-familiar pad makes things more fun.

Of course, you *don't* have closets full of beautiful china, silver, and linen. What you *do* have is imagination, ingenuity, and resourcefulness. Put those three together and you'll make every dinner guest remember not only the feast but the charming manner and place in which it was served as well.

1 TABLE LINEN: MATS, TABLECLOTHS, NAPKINS

The conventional is easy; the unique takes a bit more effort but wins you considerable extra points. For example: Why use wipe-clean plastic place mats, run-of-the-mill straw ones, or the standard linen cloth and matching napkins, when with *very little* more trouble you can set an individualistic style?

Consider shopping for fabric remnants of linen, denim, or burlap in a smashing color; or select a bold print—stripes, checks, plaids, ticking, whatever—and put together your own mats and napkins (hemmed by machine or hand, or fringed). For an evening's or weekend's work, you can pro-

There are many ways of tackling the problem of making a dinner table look memorable. The Cardinal Rule: Never apologize for what you *don't* have, or even explain! Keep chin up, smile on, eyes bright through it all. If some knives, forks, and glasses came from the dime store, it was a bold, beautiful dime store, a paragon among dime stores! Any guest who utters a snide remark about your furnishings merely reveals *his* boorishness.

A few props are needed to set the stage, and let's now see just how easy it is to acquire a nucleus of versatile objects to be used repeatedly for truly elegant, festive dining.

duce place settings at a fraction of the cost of those bought in a store.

Decide on a generous size for place mats (as large as possible depending on the size of your table), and cut the mats a half inch *larger* all around. To easy-fringe them, run two rows of machine stiching half an inch from the edge on the four sides of each mat. When you've done them all, plunk yourself in front of the TV (or your stereo) with a cool drink at your side and unravel the threads outside the stitching to make the fringe. You simply pull out the threads on each side until you reach the stitching . . . and you *can't* go any farther. This method is much simpler than hemming the edges by machine or by hand . . . although both are fine if you have the skill.

Be doubly generous in measuring the napkin size: Men and women alike adore large ones . . . nearly a lap cloth. Follow sewing procedure outlined above.

If you prefer, use different prints for each mat and napkin, or use the same print but in different color combinations for each place setting . . . a navy linen napkin with a bottle-green place mat, for example. Try navy or light blue denim mats with red bandannas for napkins.

If you want something really personal, cut up old cotton dresses and tablecloths into three-inch squares and make patchwork mats. A simple embroidery stitch, rickrack, or ribbon will cover the joining seams. Line the back with a plain linen cloth to give the mat some weight.

An ingenious Chicago hostess uses a solid brown linen tablecloth topped by an ecru lace one . . . plus brown linen napkins. Any two layers of cloth that complement each other this way are fetching. Chic idea: black felt cloth with individual place mats and napkins of black-and-white pillow ticking . . . sparked by red roses and red candles as a centerpiece. For the Christmas–New Year season why not a floor-length cloth of scarlet, green, or amethyst felt or cotton velvet, with large gold or silver round paper doilies at each place? See what *you* can dream up with upholstery trimmings, metallic braid, French ribbons. The drapery and upholstery fabrics section of a department store can be an inspiration; so can the dress goods section. *Never* overlook remnant counters. Heavy piqué or seersucker, or even cotton brocade, make luxurious mats. Even silk need not be impractical if you coat it with one of the stain repellents (such as Scotchgard) that come in spray cans. Spills and stains can be wiped off the treated surface immediately. It's a sensible precaution.

Toward having a more beautiful table, train your eye to look at objects with ingenuity. A flowered sheet doesn't have to be used *only* on a bed; it can serve as a buffet cloth if you need something large. An embroidered dresser scarf (the kind your grandmother used to *make!*) placed across the middle of a long narrow table makes a cozy setting for a *tête à tête* meal. Put flowers or candles, or both, at each end of the table . . . and your gaze, unimpeded by any centerpiece, can rest lovingly on your guest. Printed or embroidered Irish linen dish towels can be attractive mats. Brighten plain rush or straw mats by gluing on a border of French ribbon or gay felt flowers. Improvise!

Search out new table-décor ideas when you travel: a piece of mirror embroidery from Pakistan, a length of batik print from Java or Bali, a cotton sari from India, hand-screened fabrics from Puerto Rico and the Virgin Islands . . . all can inspire a new table setting. At one dinner party in San Francisco the hostess covered her dinner table with a thin off-white Turkish woolen shawl on which she'd arranged lacy straw mats bought in Cartagena, Colombia. If you only get as far as the Great Smokey Mountains, browse in the local craft shops, antique stores, flea markets. Handcrafted straw products are marvelous. Those from Charleston, South Carolina, are very different from the Cherokee Indian work of North Carolina! Wares at the Bahamian Straw Market in Nassau are not at all like the Mexican straw work in Los Angeles. An extremely talented New York hostess spent half an hour at the Tin Bazaar in Mexico City and came back 'home with the trimmings for a highly successful dinner party for twenty-four all tucked into two huge straw baskets. She bought: twenty-four tin serving plates, twenty-four tin salad or bread plates, ceramic folk-art candle holders, big paper flowers in wild colors.

Last, but hardly least, don't overlook the odds and ends that are probably lying unused and forgotten in your parents', or better still your grandparents', attic. Yesterday's white elephant may be today's *treasure!*

2 TABLE SILVER: KNIVES, FORKS, SPOONS

Yes, silver *is* a big investment. Few of us can afford to buy six place settings the moment we set up housekeeping . . . not when you consider that patterns average fifty dollars per setting. But there are ways to creep up on the sterling you covet.

First, take time to find a design you feel you can live with *forever*. Go to the finest silver stores, price anything that appeals, collect the little folders that picture the design and list the price of each piece. When you're ready to make a decision, sort the folders, eliminating any that are nice but not *special* to you. Consider your life-style, the kind of atmosphere you want to live in (modern, eighteenth century, floral, delicate) and choose the silver accordingly. There's nothing wrong with buying one or two pieces at a time; even New York's elegant Cartier, Tiffany, and Georg Jensen are happy to sell you a *single* teaspoon or salad fork. Soon you'll acquire two or three place settings *almost* painlessly. When parents and friends ask what you want for a birthday or Christmas gift, tell them your pattern and ask for a single piece. With each salary raise, buy a silver spoon. You deserve it! If someone sends a gift check, turn it into silver.

When you have enough for two, invite someone special to celebrate. Until you've actually acquired enough silver to feed a friend, select an excellent but inexpensive stainless steel flatware; most major American silversmiths offer a range of patterns, from stark modern to eighteenth-century copies with pistol-handled knives. Bargains can be had, sometimes, in Japanese import stores. Some stainless is so beautiful, and so expensive, you may *not* want to replace it.

Antique shops or fairs are another silverware source. Often odd sets are available quite reasonably. This is possibly the best way to buy serving pieces . . . meat fork, gravy ladle, serving spoons . . . none of which *really* have to match. Off-beat possibilities: Scout Chinese and Japanese stores for the lovely pottery spoons used for soup. They're *very* cheap and also are useful for serving chutney and pickles, which tarnish silver.

3 CHINA AND GLASS

Again, matching everything *isn't* necessary. Most parties are likely to be small anyway, so do pick up interesting glasses or plates or bowls in twos, or threes, or fours.

You can, of course, follow the same plan we suggested for silver: Choose a beautiful classic pattern in Wedgwood, Lenox, or Doulton china and buy one place setting at a time. Alas, by the time you *should* have completed a set for six, it's possible some of the early acquisitions may be chipped or broken. And you can ruin your disposition for a week if a guest breaks a dinner plate that costs twelve dollars to replace!

Our suggestion: Look for bargains, mix and match colors and patterns with courage and flair. Watch for china sales (usually in January, February, and September). Note that Wedgwood also makes "everyday" dinnerware . . . not only *much less* expensive than their elaborate china, but available on sale at least once a year so you can replace any broken plates or add place settings.

With regard to crystal, follow the general suggestions for china. Lovely glasses can be acquired at thrift shops. There's no *law* that says your champagne glasses *must* match cocktail or wine glasses or even each *other*. If you find only three handsome, inexpensive champagne glasses, buy them. A clever New Jersey girl made her unmatched glasses a cachet: She bought one champagne glass whenever a design intrigued her. There are *no* duplicates in her collection, and guests are charmed by the differences, picking a glass that suits them.

Country auctions can be great for some of the buys mentioned earlier. You probably won't get a dozen of anything, but who cares! Pottery-outlet stores are a bargain possibility, especially for discontinued patterns, for platters, casseroles, and serving dishes that have some tiny flaw in pattern or glaze. There is an outlet in or near most cities.

Collecting miscellany can be inspiring! The variety of the pieces will encourage you to use them in unexpected ways. For instance, you can serve

4 FLOWERS AND TABLE DECORATIONS

Flowers are traditional table decoration, but even they can be used in an unusual way. Don't limit yourself to the familiar and expensive roses or carnations. If your party is a winter one in a northern city, these blossoms probably cost as much as the groceries and wouldn't last much longer! A good way to beat the high cost of fresh flowers is to use a collection of tiny vases (no more than three inches high), perhaps five or six of them, holding only one or two small flowers and a sprig of fern, baby's breath, or a leaf. The vases needn't match. They all go in the center of the table. Save pretty perfume bottles (also a marvelous size for holding fresh flowers on a bathroom sink); reclaim your doll's tea-set from the family attic.

Chianti in those two heavy old Sandwich-glass goblets, but you can also fill them with short-stemmed flowers like nasturtiums, petunias, marigolds. Another time they might hold breadsticks, pretzels, or spears of fresh pineapple; or fill them with crushed ice as a bed for shrimp cocktail.

A gaudy piece of Victorian or art nouveau china, sprawling with nymphs and cupids or trailing vines, will enliven a setting that's *too* austere.

Sometimes it's a temptation to be safely conservative and choose stark white china, plain Scandinavian stainless flatware, dull linen mats and napkins. All of these are fine in themselves, but *en masse* the effect can be sterile.

To avoid such an austere look, you can combine vivid Mexican or Greek pottery with stainless steel; use plain white china on a brightly colored or flowered cloth.

If your linen, silver, china, and crystal are all rather conservative and don't lend themselves to exciting combinations, use fantasy and imagination in the table décor.

If you have neither time to get to a florist before the party, *nor* the budget to afford cut flowers, move a small, leafy house plant to the center of the dinner table: a pot of violets, begonias, fern. (Tie a ribbon or scarf around its rim.) A glamorous decoration can emerge from a relatively undistinguished plant if you tuck a few white or colored cut flowers among the leaves. Set the flowers in water-filled glass tubes pushed into the soil surrounding the plant, and they'll keep fresh for several days. (Note: Florists sell such tubes, or you can use plastic ones toothbrushes are packaged in.) Short-stalked flowers (roses, camellias, small chrysanthemums, or single blossoms from gladiolus or snapdragon) can be fastened to the plant with florist's wire . . . but only last one evening.

Here's another thought: Buy the smallest of red clay flowerpots in the dime store. Line each with heavy foil so it will hold water, place a pronged flower holder on the bottom, or some chicken wire, and put in mixed small fresh flowers. Have a pot at each place setting instead of one huge centerpiece.

Don't risk plastic flowers or plants unless you are very sure of your style and taste (and *very certain* of your guests' approval). However, *some* artificial flowers, such as those made of silk, beads, linen, feathers, have their own elegance. Alas, most of these are wildly expensive, too! If you want to be unconventional, even a little startling, other forms of decoration might serve the purpose even better: If there is a Mexican store handy, buy a *piñata* (one of those dangling paper sculptures of gilded and brightly colored paper filled with tiny favors) and hang it over the table. Use giant paper Mexican flowers in pots scattered around the room. At party's end open the *piñata* and out of it falls a favor.

More decorating thoughts: one of those charming Siamese mobiles, again of glittery paper, can be hung over a Far Eastern dinner setting. Or trot out your doll collection, a group of animal figurines, or some primitive wood sculpture for your centerpiece. Giant chessmen are handsome ornaments, as are beautifully mounted large shells or sea coral. A small Mexican mirror framed in tin curlicues makes a sparkling base for candles in glass or silver holders. Try an African or Balinese or Mexican wooden mask in the middle of the table, surrounded by candles in wooden candlesticks, or a *santos* . . . primitive religious carving.

Weed pots, once a luxurious item hand-crafted by talented ceramicists, are now available in practically every Japanese store at modest prices. These are short vases with tiny openings barely large enough to hold a single dried weed. Buy them in different shapes, textures, and colors, use different weeds in each, and create a handsome autumn arrangement . . . or put one pot at each place.

You are *only* limited by your imagination, young lady! Flowers can be totally replaced by centerpieces of fruit or vegetables, objects of art . . . *anything* you love. Look around!

CHAPTER 4

DINNER NUMBER 1
SERVES TWO

SUPPLY CHECKLIST
Check your supply shelf for the following; if missing any item, add to marketing list:
Flour
Rice (white, long grain)
Butter
Olive oil
Lemons
Garlic
Chicken bouillon cubes
Salt, pepper
Vermouth, dry and sweet

MARKETING LIST
1 lb. large shrimps, uncooked
1 head lettuce
1 small head escarole or curly chicory
1 bunch parsley
1 bunch fresh chives
1 lb. walnuts in the shell
1 package frozen raspberries
1 jar marinated mushrooms
1 small jar red pimentos
½ lb. Greek olives or 1 can black olives
1 bottle Soave or California dry Sémillon

MENU

VERMOUTH

GREEK OLIVES, WALNUTS

SPRINGTIME SHRIMP
GREEN RICE, MUSHROOM SALAD
ITALIAN BREAD

SOAVE

RASPBERRIES

1 PRELIMINARIES

Chill the jar of mushrooms in the refrigerator. Separate, wash, and dry salad greens by swirling them in a wire salad basket or draining on paper towels. Wrap loosely in paper towels and store in the refrigerator.

Chill the wine.

Take raspberries out of the refrigerator, and allow to thaw partially.

Shell the shrimps, and remove the veins, which are the dark threads running down the backs. Rinse and drain.

Cook $\frac{3}{4}$ c. rice according to package directions, adding 1 chicken bouillon cube, 1 tbsp. butter, and $\frac{1}{2}$ tsp. salt to the water. If rice is ready before you're through cooking the shrimps (15–20 minutes), put a folded towel or several layers of paper towels under the lid, and leave the pan at back of stove to keep rice fluffy.

2 PREPARING THE MAIN DISH

INGREDIENTS:
1 lb. shrimps, raw, shelled, and deveined
2 tbsp. flour
2 tbsp. olive oil
3 tbsp. butter ($\frac{3}{8}$ of one stick)
1 tsp. lemon juice
1 tsp. finely minced garlic
2 tbsp. minced parsley
$\frac{1}{2}$ c. hot water

METHOD:

Dust the shrimps with 1 tbsp. flour. Melt 1 tbsp. of butter with the 2 tbsp. olive oil in a flat baking tin. Arrange shrimps evenly in tin, and broil under a low flame 3 inches from the heat for 8 minutes. Make the sauce while the shrimps are cooking. Melt 1 tbsp. butter in a small saucepan. Stir in 1 tbsp. flour; then add hot water, lemon juice, and a dash of salt and pepper. Bring to the boil, and cook for 5 minutes, stirring with a small whisk. Stir in the remaining 1 tbsp. of butter, and add the garlic and parsley. Take the pan of shrimps from under the broiler, pour the sauce over them, and stir so that they are all well coated. Raise the broiler heat to high, and put the shrimps back to broil for 2–3 minutes. You may find it easier to postpone final cooking until after you fix the salad, season the rice, and serve the predinner drinks. That way the shrimps will be piping hot without being overcooked.

3 FINAL ASSEMBLY

Drain the liquid from the marinated mushrooms, and toss it with the salad greens in a bowl. Garnish with the mushrooms and a little chopped pimento.

Fluff the rice with a fork. Add 2 tbsp. each chopped parsley and chopped chives.

Wrap the Italian bread in foil and warm 10 minutes in a 400° oven. Cut or tear it into chunks.

4 SERVING THE DINNER

Pour the vermouth, 1 jigger of dry and 1 jigger of sweet to each portion, over ice cubes, and garnish with a thin twist of lemon peel. Pass the Greek olives and a bowl of fresh walnuts in their shells as cocktail snacks. Don't forget nutcrackers!

For the main course, serve the shrimps and green rice on warmed plates, along with the bowl of mushroom salad. Pour the wine.

Dessert: partially thawed raspberries in individual bowls with 1 or 2 tsp. liqueur over each portion. Use Grand Marnier, Cointreau, Curaçao, or a similar fruit-flavored liqueur if you have it—glamorous but not essential.

DINNER NUMBER 2
SERVES TWO

SUPPLY CHECKLIST
Check your supply shelf for the following; if missing any item, add to marketing list:

Butter
Olive oil
Mayonnaise
Garlic
Lemons
Vodka
Dry vermouth
Salt, pepper
Basil

MARKETING LIST
1 large raw lobster, about 2 lbs., split in half
1 lb. crisp, red apples
1 bunch parsley
Basil, fresh or dried (or oregano)
1 package Italian-style frozen green beans
2 medium eggs (*not* large ones)
1 box Camembert cheese, preferably fresh from a cheese store, not the supermarket dairy-case kind
½ lb. spaghettini
1 package wheat wafers or other plain crackers
1 French bread, preferably the long thin type
1 15-oz. can marinara sauce
1 very small jar red (salmon) caviar
1 dill pickle
1 bottle Sauvignon Blanc or similar American dry white wine

MENU

VODKA MARTINI

RUSSIAN EGGS

LOBSTER FRA DIAVOLO
BUTTERED SPAGHETTINI
ITALIAN-STYLE GREEN BEANS
FRENCH BREAD

SAUVIGNON BLANC

CRISP RED APPLES
CAMEMBERT

1 PRELIMINARIES

Take Camembert cheese out of the refrigerator and let it come to room temperature. Chill the wine. Cover the eggs with cold water in a small pan, and add 2 tbsp. salt to help prevent white from leaking out if eggs should crack in cooking. Bring to boil, and simmer for 10 minutes. Drain and run cold water over them.

When eggs are cold, shell and cut in half lengthwise. Arrange flat side down on two small plates, spoon 1 tbsp. of mayonnaise over each half, and decorate the top of each with $\frac{1}{2}$ tsp. red caviar. Garnish the plates with two dill pickle slices and a parsley sprig. Keep cool in the refrigerator until serving time.

2 PREPARING THE MAIN DISH

INGREDIENTS:

1 raw lobster, split in half	2 tbsp. minced parsley
4 tbsp. olive oil	$\frac{1}{2}$ tsp. basil or oregano, chopped or
Salt, pepper	crushed fine
1 clove garlic, minced	1 can marinara sauce

METHOD:

Heat 3 tbsp. olive oil in a large skillet, and sauté the lobster, cut sides down, for 5 minutes. Turn and top with the other ingredients, adding marinara sauce last. Add water to the skillet to the depth of $\frac{1}{4}$ inch, cover, and steam for 45 minutes over a low heat. When the lobster has been cooking about 20 minutes, prepare spaghettini according to package directions, adding salt and 1 tbsp. oil to the cooking water. (The oil prevents sticking together.) When lobster is tender but not mushy, drain and add 2–3 tbsp. butter, stirring to mix it well.

Cook Italian-style green beans, drain, and sprinkle beans with lemon juice.

Wrap the French bread in foil and warm it (about 10 minutes) until crisp in a 400° oven.

3 SERVING THE DINNER

Chill martini glasses and pitcher. If your guest prides himself on his skill as a bartender, ask him if he would like to mix the drinks. If *you* do the honors, stir 5 parts gin and 1 part dry vermouth with ice cubes, and serve on the rocks or straight up, with a twist of thinly pared lemon peel.

Serve Russian egg appetizer.

For the main course, serve lobster, spaghettini, and green beans on warmed plates with a basket of French bread chunks. Provide lobster-cracking tools if available, or a nutcracker, which works just as well. Tiny seafood or pickle forks are useful for extracting the last delicious bite of meat from lobster claws. Have plenty of paper napkins handy—lobster enjoyment can be *messy.*

Pour the wine.

Dessert: Camembert cheese, wheat wafers, and a bowl of shiny red apples.

DINNER NUMBER 3
SERVES TWO

SUPPLY CHECKLIST
Check your supply shelf for the following; if missing any item, add to marketing list:
Rice (white, long grain)
Butter
Dried rosemary leaves
Parsley flakes
Chicken bouillon cubes
Salt, pepper

MARKETING LIST
1 lb. chicken livers
1 ripe cantaloupe
2 tomatoes
2 large or 4 small heads endive
1 small head romaine
1 lime
1 package bake-and-serve hard rolls
1 frozen cheesecake
1 bottle Roquefort dressing
1 bottle dry sherry (Spanish Tio Pepe or La Ina, or California Almadén)
1 bottle Beaujolais or Zinfandel (California red wine)

MENU

DRY SHERRY

ICED CANTALOUPE

CHICKEN LIVERS VIN ROUGE
RICE PILAF, BELGIAN ENDIVE

HARD ROLLS

BEAUJOLAIS

CHEESECAKE

1 PRELIMINARIES

Break off a few leaves from the head of romaine. Wash, dry, and arrange them on salad plates. Remove outer leaves from endive. Slice in circles and arrange them on the romaine leaves. Put in the refrigerator until serving time.

Allow cheesecake to defrost at room temperature.

Cook $\frac{3}{4}$ c. rice according to package directions, adding 1 chicken bouillon cube and $\frac{1}{2}$ tsp. salt to the water.

Bake the hard rolls according to package directions.

Uncork the wine at least an hour before dinner to allow the wine to "breathe." Only red wines need this treatment.

2 PREPARING THE MAIN DISH

INGREDIENTS:
1 lb. chicken livers
2 tbsp. butter
2 medium tomatoes, cut in small chunks

$\frac{1}{4}$ **to** $\frac{1}{2}$ **c. dry red wine**
Dash salt, pepper
$\frac{1}{2}$ **tsp. dried rosemary leaves**

METHOD:

Rinse and dry chicken livers, and cut each in half. Melt butter in a skillet. When hot, add livers, browning them quickly over a medium-high flame. Add the rest of the ingredients, and bring to a boil. Reduce heat and simmer 5–7 minutes. The livers should be faintly pink in the center.

3 SERVING THE DINNER

Serve sherry in small wineglasses or on the rocks in old-fashioned glasses.

Serve cantaloupe halves with sections of lime to squeeze over them.

For the main course, arrange chicken livers in the middle of a mound of rice pilaf. Garnish with a sprinkle of parsley flakes. Spoon well-shaken Roquefort dressing over endive salad, 1 or 2 tbsp. to each portion.

Pour wine.

Dessert: wedges of cheesecake.

DINNER NUMBER 4
SERVES FOUR

SUPPLY CHECKLIST
Check your supply shelf for the following; if missing any item, add to marketing list:

Butter
Powdered sugar
Powdered ginger
Tabasco
Worcestershire sauce
French or Italian dressing
Salt, cayenne
Dry mustard
Garlic powder

MARKETING LIST
2 lbs. ham slice, precooked, 1 inch thick
Salad greens: lettuce (Boston, Bibb, or iceberg)
    watercress
    escarole, chicory, or romaine
1 large fresh pineapple, or 2 small ones
1 package instant mashed yams
1 jar orange marmalade
1 package shelled almonds
1 medium can clam juice
1 medium can tomato juice
$\frac{1}{2}$ dozen bakery muffins
1 six-pack beer (or more, to be on the safe side) or
2 quart-bottles hard cider
1 small bottle Grand Marnier
1 small bottle kirsch (Grand Marnier or rum may be substituted)

MENU

ICED TOMATO-AND-CLAM JUICE
DEVILED ALMONDS

HAM SLICE FLAMBÉ
MASHED YAMS, TOSSED GREEN SALAD
MUFFINS

BEER OR HARD CIDER

FRESH PINEAPPLE

1 PRELIMINARIES

Chill beer or cider in the refrigerator, as well as clam juice and tomato juice. Take the brown peel off the almonds by putting them in a small pan of boiling water, removing it from the heat, and allowing to stand for a few minutes. The skins will slip off easily. Melt 2 tbsp. butter in a skillet. When butter is hot, put in almonds, and sprinkle with 1 tsp. salt and $\frac{1}{4}$ tsp. cayenne (more if you like, but it's *very* pungent). Add a dash of Worcestershire sauce, and a tiny pinch of garlic powder if you like garlic. Stir over a medium heat until slightly browned.

Prepare fresh pineapple by peeling it and cutting out all brown thorny tufts. Remove hard core and slice fruit in rounds or lengthwise sticks. Arrange in a flat serving dish, and sprinkle with 2 tbsp. powdered sugar. Add a jigger of kirsch. (If you don't have kirsch, a jigger of Grand Marnier or rum will do.) Put in refrigerator to chill.

Wash salad greens, drain, and pat dry with paper towels, or toss in a salad basket. Wrap in paper towels and store in the refrigerator until you are ready to prepare the salad.

2 PREPARING THE MAIN DISH

INGREDIENTS:
- 2 lbs. ham slice
- $\frac{1}{2}$ c. orange marmalade
- $\frac{1}{4}$ tsp. Worcestershire sauce
- $\frac{1}{2}$ tsp. dry mustard
- $\frac{1}{4}$ tsp. powdered ginger
- 2 drops Tabasco
- 4 tbsp. Grand Marnier

METHOD:

Slash fat around the edges of the ham to prevent curling, and place on a baking-serving platter. Mix the orange marmalade, Worcestershire sauce, mustard, ginger, and Tabasco to a paste. Spread over the top of the ham, and bake in a 350° oven for about 30 minutes until glaze is brown and shiny.

While the ham is baking, prepare the mashed yams according to package directions. Tear the salad greens into bite-size pieces, put them into a salad bowl, and toss with about $\frac{1}{4}$ c. of French or Italian dressing. Wrap muffins in foil, and heat for 10 minutes in the oven. Chill glasses for the tomato-and-clam juice.

Warm the Grand Marnier in a small saucepan, ignite, and pour flaming over the ham. Serve while still flaming. This step, of course, should be done at the very last minute; in fact, if your kitchen is more than a few steps from the dining table, it's better to do the flaming right at the table. Be very careful!

3 SERVING THE DINNER

First pour tomato-and-clam juice, mixed half and half, into chilled glasses. Accompany with deviled almonds served in a dish lined with a paper doily or napkin, or in a wooden bowl.

For the main course flame and serve ham with the mashed yams. Bring out the salad bowl. Put out basket of hot muffins.

Pour beer or cider.

Dessert: fresh pineapple sticks.

DINNER NUMBER 5
SERVES TWO

Check your supply shelf for the following; if missing any item, add to marketing list:

Rice (white, long grain, not instant)
Olive oil
Butter
Sliced almonds
Raisins
Curry powder
Caraway seeds
Salt, pepper
Lemon (1)
Dietary liquid sweetener

MARKETING LIST
4 1-inch-thick pork chops, about
      $1\frac{1}{4}$ lbs.
1 bunch scallions (green onions)
1 bunch watercress
1 bunch parsley or chives
1 large onion, Bermuda or red
1 package frozen broccoli
2 large oranges
1 8-oz. can tomato sauce
1 pint lemon sherbet
$\frac{1}{2}$ pint light cream (optional)
1 loaf dark rye bread, unsliced
1 small bottle cassis (black currant)
      liqueur
1 bottle vodka
1 bottle Pinot Blanc or Rhine wine
      (dry white wine)
1 box vanilla wafers
1 can vichyssoise

MENU

BALTIC COCKTAIL

CHILLED VICHYSSOISE

PORK CHOPS SENEGALESE
BROCCOLI SPRIGS, ORANGE-ONION SALAD
DARK RYE BREAD

PINOT BLANC

LEMON SHERBET

1 PRELIMINARIES

Crush and bruise $\frac{1}{4}$ tsp. caraway seeds, preferably using a small pestle and mortar. If you don't have these, chop and crush the seeds with a knife. Put them in a screw-top jar, and cover with $\frac{3}{4}$ c. vodka. Add 2 or 3 drops dietary liquid sweetener. Refrigerate, overnight if possible.

Chill the vichyssoise and the white wine until serving.

To prepare salad: Take off outer peels and inner white piths of the oranges. Remove any seeds, slice fruit $\frac{1}{2}$ inch thick in circles, and arrange on a platter. Over orange slices put rings of very thinly sliced onion. Sprinkle with grated black pepper and 1 tbsp. olive oil. Garnish with watercress sprigs. Chill in refrigerator until serving time.

2 PREPARING THE MAIN DISH

INGREDIENTS:

- 4 pork chops
- $\frac{2}{3}$ c. uncooked rice
- $\frac{1}{2}$ c. raisins
- $\frac{1}{2}$ c. sliced almonds
- 2 green onions, chopped
- $\frac{1}{2}$ tsp. curry powder
- 1 8-oz. can tomato sauce
- 1 c. dry white wine
- $\frac{1}{2}$ tsp. salt

METHOD:

Trim any excess fat off the chops. Sprinkle salt in the bottom of a large skillet (one with a lid). Heat the skillet, put in the chops, and brown them on both sides. In a bowl combine rice, raisins, almonds, green onions, and curry powder. Spoon this mixture around and over the chops. Then mix the tomato sauce with the wine, and pour over meat. Bring to a boil. Reduce heat, cover, and allow to simmer gently for 30 minutes (or until the rice is tender).

3 FINAL ASSEMBLY

While chops are cooking, prepare broccoli according to directions on package. Drain carefully, add a pat of butter to the broccoli, and keep warm in double boiler over hot water until serving time.

Cut rye bread in thick slices, and divide each slice in four. Arrange in a basket.

Put chilled vichyssoise in soup cups, swirl a spoonful of cream in each (optional), and sprinkle with a little chopped parsley or chives.

Put the skillet containing the chops on an asbestos pad over a very low flame so the contents will keep hot without overcooking.

4 SERVING THE DINNER

For the Baltic cocktail, put ice cubes into an old-fashioned glass, add a twist of lemon peel, and strain in the flavored vodka. Add a splash of water or club soda if desired.

Serve chilled vichyssoise.

For the main course, serve pork chops Senegalese with buttered broccoli. Put out the salad and the rye bread.

Pour the chilled white wine; use large wineglasses, fill three quarters full.

Dessert: Scoop lemon sherbet into dessert bowls, and pour ½ jigger of cassis over each. Crème de menthe, Kahlúa, or a similar liqueur may be substituted. If you don't have liqueur, dilute ¼ c. apricot or black currant jam with a little orange or lemon juice for a delicious topping.

DINNER NUMBER 6
SERVES TWO

Check your supply shelf for the following; if missing any item, add to marketing list:

Cornstarch
Butter
Olive oil
Wine vinegar
Dried tarragon
Salt, pepper
Vermouth, dry and sweet
Angostura bitters
Egg (1)

MARKETING LIST

2 Rock Cornish hens, approx. 1 lb. each
1 bunch parsley
1 bunch green onions
1 1-pint basket strawberries
1 jar or can green asparagus spears or 1 package frozen asparagus spears
1 small carton sour cream
1 package heat-and-serve croissants
1 package wild rice
1 pint strawberry ice cream or sherbet
1 can consommé madrilene
1 bottle dry sherry (New York State or California)
1 bottle Tavel (French) or Grenache (California) rosé wine

MENU

SHERRY COCKTAIL

JELLIED MADRILENE

SHERRIED ROCK CORNISH GAME HENS
WILD RICE, COLD ASPARAGUS
CROISSANTS

TAVEL ROSÉ

STRAWBERRY ICE CREAM

1 PRELIMINARIES

Put the canned madrilene in the refrigerator to chill thoroughly, preferably the night before the dinner. Don't put it in the freezing compartment; the texture will be spoiled.

If you buy frozen asparagus, cook it ahead of time until just tender. Drain juices and chill. Canned asparagus should be drained very carefully and chilled. Make the ravigote dressing as follows: Put 1 egg (in shell) into a small saucepan. Cover with cold water, and add 2 tbsp. salt. Bring to the boil, and simmer 10 minutes. Cool the egg, shell, and chop finely. In a screw-top jar, mix 5 tbsp. oil, 2 tbsp. vinegar, 1 tsp. salt, and a dash of black pepper. Shake until blended. Add 1 tbsp. chopped parsley, 1 tsp. chopped green onion, and the chopped hard-boiled egg. Chill in the refrigerator.

Wash and stem a dozen strawberries, chill them.

2 PREPARING THE MAIN DISH

INGREDIENTS:

2 Rock Cornish game hens
Salt, pepper
1 stick butter ($\frac{1}{4}$ lb.)
1 c. dry sherry
$\frac{1}{2}$ tsp. dried tarragon
2 tsp. cornstarch

METHOD:

Take the necks and giblets out of the birds. Rinse the cavities and the outsides, and pat dry with paper towels. Sprinkle inside and out with a little salt and pepper. Melt butter in a shallow roasting pan. Put birds into pan, pour 2 tbsp. sherry over each, then brown them on all sides over medium heat on top of stove. Add the tarragon to the rest of the sherry, pour over the birds in the pan, and roast them, uncovered, in a 350° oven 45–60 minutes. Baste three or four times with the juices in the pan. (A squeeze-bulb baster makes this job easier.)

When the birds have been cooking for 45 minutes, check to see if they are well browned. If they are still too pale, raise the heat to 400° for the last 10 minutes of cooking.

Remove the cooked birds from the baking pan, and keep in a warm place. Mix cornstarch to a smooth, thin paste with a little cold water. Add to the juices in the pan, bring to a boil on top of the stove, and stir the entire mixture until the sauce is shiny and thick.

3 FINAL ASSEMBLY

While the birds are cooking, prepare wild rice according to package directions.

Spoon jellied madrilene into soup cups or small bowls, breaking it up a little and mounding to a peak with a fork. Place a dollop of sour cream (about 1 tbsp.) on top of each portion, add a bit of chopped parsley. Leave in the refrigerator until the moment of serving—you don't want it to melt in a hot kitchen while you drink your cocktails.

Make the sherry cocktail in a shaker or pitcher. Use 3 jiggers sherry, 2 dry vermouth, 1 sweet vermouth, and a dash of Angostura bitters. Stir or shake with ice cubes.

Heat the croissants in the oven according to package directions.

4 SERVING THE DINNER

Strain the sherry cocktail into cold glasses (on the rocks or straight up, whichever you prefer), and serve with a twist of lemon peel if desired.

Serve the jellied madrilene.

For the main course, serve the Rock Cornish hens with wild rice on warmed plates, along with the sauce in a separate bowl or gravy boat.

Shake the ravigote dressing; pour over the chilled asparagus on salad plates, and serve.

Pour the rosé wine.

Dessert: strawberry ice cream or sherbet surrounded by a ring of whole fresh berries.

DINNER NUMBER 7
SERVES TWO

Flour
Butter
Mayonnaise
Grated Parmesan or Romano cheese
French dressing or oil and vinegar
Lemons
Nutmeg
Tabasco
Vermouth, dry and sweet
Angostura bitters
Salt, pepper
Olive oil

MARKETING LIST
1 lb. sole fillets (2 large or 4 medium)
2 10-oz. packages frozen chopped
     spinach
1 bag frozen tiny potatoes or 1 can
     new potatoes
1 lb. firm ripe tomatoes
1 bunch parsley
1 large ripe avocado
1 small can pâté de foie, 4–6 oz.
1 can truffles (smallest size)
1 can date-nut loaf
1 package bake-and-serve hard rolls
1 package melba toast rounds
1 pint vanilla ice cream
1 bottle Chenin Blanc or Chablis
     wine
1 small bottle Scotch whiskey
1 small bottle brandy

MENU

ROB ROY

PÂTÉ DE FOIE
MELBA TOAST ROUNDS

FILLET OF SOLE FLORENTINE
POTATOES RISSOLÉES
AVOCADO-TOMATO SALAD
HARD ROLLS

CHENIN BLANC

DATE-NUT CAKE

1 PRELIMINARIES

Open can of pâté de foie, and turn it over into a small bowl. Mash pâté with a fork, and add 1 tbsp. brandy and 1 or 2 drops Tabasco. Add 1 tsp. finely chopped truffle (1 small truffle or $\frac{1}{2}$ large one) and mix well. Press the pâté into two very small dishes (individual soufflé molds or ramekins are good if you have them; otherwise use foil baking cups set in a muffin tin to hold their shape). Chill in the refrigerator for at least several hours before your guest arrives.

Prepare salad. Slice tomatoes into rings $\frac{1}{4}$ inch to $\frac{1}{2}$ inch thick. Peel avocado, cut in quarters and then in eighths. Arrange alternate slices of tomato and avocado; sprinkle with a few drops of lemon juice to prevent discoloration. Cover with plastic wrap, and chill in the refrigerator.

Chill white wine in the refrigerator.

2 PREPARING THE MAIN DISH

INGREDIENTS:

1 bag frozen tiny potatoes or 1 can new potatoes
2 large or 4 medium sole fillets
Flour
Salt, pepper

2 tbsp. butter
2 10-oz. packages frozen spinach
2 tbsp. dry white wine
4 tbsp. mayonnaise
2–4 tsp. grated cheese

METHOD:

First start the potatoes. Choose 10 or 12 potatoes about the same size. (If you are using the frozen kind, put them into a pan, and pour boiling water over them to thaw them. Allow to stand for ten minutes; then drain and dry.) Put 1 tbsp. oil and 1 tbsp. butter into a skillet or saucepan, and when the butter has melted, add potatoes and cook slowly with the lid on for 10–15 minutes. Shake pan frequently to brown potatoes evenly. Take off lid and continue cooking for about another 5 minutes until the potatoes are golden brown and cooked through. Canned potatoes need only about 5 minutes to brown, as they are already cooked.

Prepare fish fillets by rinsing under running water. Season flour with a little salt and pepper, and dip fillets in it, pressing to coat evenly, shaking off any excess. Melt butter in a large skillet and sauté fish until golden on each side. If the pan isn't large enough for all the fillets to lie flat without overlapping, do them in two batches, adding a little more butter for the second batch.

While the fish cooks, prepare the spinach. Drain spinach very carefully; otherwise the finished dish will look watery. Season spinach with a grating of nutmeg (whole nutmegs keep their flavor much better than the ready-ground kind). Spread spinach in a flat oven-to-table baking dish, preferably oval or oblong. Heat the bake-and-serve rolls in the oven—they will take longer than the final stages of preparing the fish.

When spinach has cooled a little, arrange the fish fillets side by side on top, and sprinkle with the white wine. Add a dash of salt and pepper, and spread the mayonnaise evenly over the surface of the fish. Sprinkle with grated cheese, and put under the broiler, 3 inches from the flame, until well heated and glazed (about 3–4 minutes). You may find it easier to keep the fish dish in a cool oven, 250°, while you serve the drinks and appetizer, and to put it under the broiler, at high heat, for a few minutes just before serving.

3 FINAL ASSEMBLY

Cut 1-inch slices of date-nut loaf, and put on dessert plates.

Sprinkle salad with 2–3 tbsp. of French or Italian dressing.

Chill cocktail glasses. Prepare two Rob Roy cocktails by mixing, in a shaker or pitcher, 3 jiggers Scotch with 1 jigger each dry vermouth and sweet vermouth. Add a dash of Angostura bitters to the shaker, and stir.

4 SERVING THE DINNER

Serve cocktails on the rocks or straight up with a twist of lemon peel.

Arrange the pâté in its individual container on a small plate, garnished with a tiny parsley sprig and accompanied by melba toast rounds.

For the main course, serve the sole Florentine, with the potatoes rissolées arranged around it. Bring out the avocado-tomato salad. Arrange rolls in a basket or on a tray.

Pour the wine.

Dessert: date-nut loaf with a scoop of ice cream on top.

DINNER NUMBER 8
SERVES TWO

MENU

DRY MARTINI

CRUDITÉS

PORK CHOPS NEW ORLEANS
MIXED GREEN SALAD
BREADSTICKS

BORDEAUX

GINGER-APPLE SNOW

SUPPLY LIST
Check your supply shelf for the following; if missing any item, add to marketing list:

Butter
Mayonnaise
Ketchup
Worcestershire sauce
Egg (1)
Chicken bouillon cubes
Dry sage
Dry thyme
Dry mustard
Salt, pepper
Gin
Dry vermouth
Tabasco
Rice (white, long grain)

MARKETING LIST
4 pork chops, $\frac{3}{4}$ inch thick, about 1$\frac{1}{4}$ lbs.
1 lb. tomatoes
1 lb. onions
1 bunch carrots
1 head lettuce
1 bunch escarole or curly chicory, or two endives
1 bunch watercress
1 small cauliflower
1 bunch celery
1 cucumber
1 green pepper
$\frac{1}{2}$ pint whipping cream
1 bottle Roquefort dressing
1 8-oz. can or jar applesauce
1 package plain cookies or wafers
1 box breadsticks, plain or with sesame seeds
1 small package candied ginger or dry ginger
1 bottle Bordeaux or other dry red wine

1 PRELIMINARIES

Trim leaves and bottom of stalk from cauliflower, and remove any brown or bruised patches. Soak upside down in a bowl of salted cold water for about an hour. Cut off 8 or 10 small even-sized sprigs (save the rest of the cauliflower for another meal). Break off 3 or 4 unbruised white stalks of celery, wash carefully, and cut into 2-inch lengths. Wash the cucumber, score the green peel lengthwise with the tines of a fork, and cut off about a dozen $\frac{1}{2}$-inch slices. Peel or scrape 2 large carrots, and cut into strips the size of shoestring potatoes. Wrap all the vegetables in clean paper towels, and put them in the vegetable crisper compartment of the refrigerator.

Make the dipping sauce as follows: Mix $\frac{1}{2}$ tsp. dry mustard with a little water. Add to $\frac{1}{2}$ c. mayonnaise and 2–3 tbsp. ketchup. Beat with a spoon or whisk, add $\frac{1}{2}$ tsp. Worcestershire sauce and a dash or two of Tabasco. Cover the bowl with plastic wrap, and chill in the refrigerator. Wash and dry some lettuce, watercress, escarole, chicory, or endive on paper towels or in a salad basket. Wrap in paper towels, and store in the refrigerator.

Uncork the wine about an hour before dinner so it will be well-aired when you serve it.

2 PREPARING THE MAIN DISH

INGREDIENTS:

4 pork chops	Salt, pepper
2 tomatoes, sliced	$\frac{2}{3}$ c. uncooked rice
1 large onion, sliced	1 c. chicken broth (made with bouillon cube)
1 green pepper, chopped	$\frac{1}{2}$ c. dry red wine
$\frac{1}{4}$ tsp. thyme	
$\frac{1}{4}$ tsp. sage	

METHOD:

Cut off almost all the fat from the pork chops. Cut the fat into little pieces, and fry them very gently in a large skillet without any oil. Skim remaining pieces of fat, leaving liquid fat in the pan. Brown the chops on both sides in this liquid. Place them in a large casserole. Arrange over them the sliced tomato, onion, and green pepper. Sprinkle with the thyme, sage, and a little salt and pepper. Scatter the uncooked rice on top of meat and vegetables. In a separate pan, heat the chicken broth and wine together, and pour over the rice in the casserole. Cover the casserole and bake in a 350° oven for ¾ hour, or until the rice is fully cooked and has soaked up the liquid.

While the main dish is cooking, prepare the dessert. Chill a mixing bowl and beater or wire whisk by putting it in the freezer. Open the applesauce, and put it through a fine strainer to drain any excess juice. If you have candied ginger, chop it finely (there should be about 2 tbsp.) Whip the cream in the chilled bowl until it holds its shape. In another bowl, mix the drained applesauce, the ginger (if candied ginger is not available, flavor the applesauce with ½ tsp. powdered *dry* ginger mixed with 1 tbsp. sugar), and half of the whipped cream. Refrigerate the bowls of cream and applesauce mixture.

3 FINAL ASSEMBLY

Tear salad greens into bite-size pieces; if endive is used, cut in ½-inch slices. Arrange in salad bowl, and chill.

Arrange the cauliflower, carrot, celery, and cucumber around a platter with a small bowl of the dipping sauce in the middle.

Whip the white of 1 egg *very stiff,* using a copper bowl if you have one. (This will be added to the applesauce last.

4 SERVING THE DINNER

If your guest is choosy about his martinis, and you have premium gin to make them with, give him the option of being bartender. If he says no, *you* do it. Mix 5 parts gin to 1 part dry vermouth, stirring in a pitcher with ice cubes. Serve in well-chilled glasses with a cocktail olive or a twist of lemon.

Serve the crudités and dipping sauce with the cocktails.

For the main course, bring the pork chops to the table in the casserole. Pour about 3 tbsp. of Roquefort dressing over the salad greens; toss together at the table. Serve the breadsticks in a basket or standing up in a large pewter beer mug. Pour the wine.

Dessert: Stir the stiffly beaten egg white into the ginger-apple-cream mixture. Divide into two dessert dishes, and top each with a dollop of whipped cream. Serve with plain cookies or wafers.

DINNER NUMBER 9
SERVES TWO

SUPPLY CHECKLIST
Check your supply shelf for the following; if missing any item, add to marketing list:

Butter
Prepared mustard, preferably Dijon
      type
Dry vermouth
Orange bitters
Small, thin skewers, wooden or metal
Lemon

MARKETING LIST
1 ham steak, $\frac{3}{4}$ inch thick, 1–1$\frac{1}{2}$ lb.
1 small lettuce (Boston, Bibb, or Ruby)
1 bunch parsley
1 package frozen broccoli spears
1–1$\frac{1}{2}$ lb. medium-size yams or sweet
      potatoes
1 package bake-and-serve butterflake
      rolls
1 jar marinated mushrooms
1 can chicken broth or chicken
      bouillon cubes
1 jar apple butter
1 small jar red currant jelly
1 can or jar babas au rhum
1 package raisins, seeded if available
1 bottle New York state or California
      sherry, medium dry
1 bottle rosé wine or domestic dry
      champagne

MENU

REFORM CLUB SHERRY COCKTAIL

MUSHROOMS À LA GRECQUE

HAM STEAK NEW ORLEANS
BAKED YAMS, BROCCOLI SPEARS
BUTTERFLAKE ROLLS

ROSÉ WINE

BABAS AU RHUM

1 PRELIMINARIES

Chill the champagne or rosé wine well in the refrigerator. Wash and dry the lettuce in a salad basket or on paper towels, and arrange 2 or 3 leaves flat on each of two small plates. Drain the mushrooms and thread them on four short skewers. Lay two skewers on each lettuce-lined plate, sprinkle with a little chopped parsley, and refrigerate until serving time.

Heat the oven to 350°. Scrub 4 medium-size yams, and make 2 small slits on top of each with a sharp-pointed knife so they don't burst while baking. Put yams in the oven to bake; they do better directly on the rack than in a baking tin. If you don't have a second rack, fit them in the corners of the rack you will put the casserole on to bake.

2 PREPARING THE MAIN DISH

INGREDIENTS:

- 1 **ham steak**
- $\frac{1}{2}$ **c. chicken broth**
- $\frac{1}{4}$ **c. apple butter**
- $\frac{1}{4}$ **c. sherry**
- 1 **tbsp. red currant jelly**
- $\frac{1}{2}$ **tsp. prepared mustard**
- 2 **tbsp. raisins**

METHOD:

Slash edges of ham steak to prevent curling, and place in baking dish. Combine all other ingredients in a saucepan, stir, and simmer for 5 minutes. Pour them over the ham steak, covering the meat evenly. Put the dish, uncovered, in the oven to bake for approximately 1 hour, until tender and glazed.

While the ham is cooking, prepare the frozen broccoli according to package directions. Drain carefully, and keep broccoli warm over hot water until serving time.

Heat the butterflake rolls according to package directions. About 15 or 20 minutes before the ham is finished, check to see if the yams are soft. If they are fully cooked, take them out of the oven, and wrap them in a towel or napkin to keep warm. Unwrap and put them back in the oven to reheat slightly while you serve the drinks and appetizer. Yams usually take about an hour, depending on size.

3 FINAL ASSEMBLY

Arrange babas on small dessert plates, pouring a little syrup over them.

Make the Reform Club cocktail as follows: Stir with ice ½ c. sherry, ¼ c. dry vermouth, and 2 dashes orange bitters. Strain into chilled glasses, and garnish with a twist of lemon.

4 SERVING THE DINNER

Serve the cocktails and the mushroom appetizer.

For the main course, arrange ham on a large serving platter. Make a slit in the yams, and tuck a pat of butter in each one. Put yams and broccoli around the ham, and bring to the table.

Put the butterflake rolls in a basket. Pour the wine or champagne.

Dessert: babas au rhum.

DINNER NUMBER 10
SERVES TWO

SUPPLY CHECKLIST
Check your supply shelf for the following; if missing any item, add to marketing list:

Butter
Worcestershire sauce
Cayenne
Curry powder
Whiskey (blended, Scotch, or bourbon)
Salt
Lemon

MARKETING LIST
½ lb. bacon
12 jumbo shrimps, uncooked, about
    1 lb.
1 bunch green onions
1 or 2 large thin-skinned oranges
1 large ripe avocado
1 red apple
1 package rice pilaf
1 package Pilot crackers
1 can vegetable-beef soup
1 package fortune cookies or
    brown-edged wafers
1 pint raspberry sherbet
1 bottle Tahitian salad dressing
1 bottle soy sauce
1 bottle chutney or Chinese sweet-
    and-sour sauce
1 bottle California or imported
    Riesling wine

MENU

WHISKEY SOUR

MULLIGATAWNY SOUP

POLYNESIAN SHRIMP
RICE PILAF, ORANGE-AVOCADO SALAD
DEVILED CRACKERS

ALSATIAN OR CALIFORNIA RIESLING

RASPBERRY SHERBET

1 PRELIMINARIES

Chill the wine in the refrigerator.

Wash the green onions, cut off roots, and take off any dry or bruised outside layers. Put aside 6 of the larger ones for the shrimp dish. Chop enough of the remaining ones to make 1 tbsp. Peel and core the apple, and dice half of it. Melt 2 tbsp. butter in a saucepan, and sauté the chopped onion and apple over low heat until soft. Stir in 1 tbsp. curry powder, and cook a few minutes longer. Add the canned soup and $1\frac{1}{4}$ c. water. Stir, and simmer 5 minutes. Set aside, covered, until time to serve the soup course.

Prepare deviled crackers as follows:

Melt 2 tbsp. butter in a small pan, and add $\frac{1}{2}$ tsp. Worcestershire sauce. Brush mixture lightly over both sides of 10 or 12 Pilot crackers, sprinkle with salt and a very little cayenne. Arrange on a large, flat baking tin or cookie sheet, and crisp in a moderate (350°) oven until golden brown . . . about 5–6 minutes.

Prepare salad. Peel off skins and piths from oranges, and cut fruit in $\frac{1}{2}$-inch rings. Peel avocado, and cut into 8 sections. Alternate slices of avocado and orange on a salad platter, sprinkling the avocado with a little orange juice to avoid discoloration. Chill in refrigerator.

2 PREPARING THE MAIN DISH

INGREDIENTS:

12 raw jumbo shrimps, shelled and deveined
$\frac{1}{4}$ c. soy sauce

6 green onions
6 slices bacon, cut in half

METHOD:

Shell and devein shrimps, and rinse them. Pat dry with paper towels. Put in a bowl and pour soy sauce over them. Stir well, and let stand 5–10 minutes.

Cut most of the top off each green onion, so that remaining sections are about 3 inches long. Split each onion in half. Lay a piece of green onion on each shrimp, and wrap in half a slice of bacon. Secure with a toothpick.

Start rice pilaf according to package directions before cooking shrimp, as the rice takes slightly longer.

Arrange shrimps in a flat baking

pan. Broil under high heat 3 inches from flame for 8–10 minutes, turning once.

Shrimps should be pink and bacon should be crisp.

3 FINAL ASSEMBLY

Reheat soup on very low flame.

Prepare whiskey sour: The usual proportion is 2 jiggers whiskey to the juice of ½ lemon, and ½ tsp. sugar for each drink, but you may prefer it with more sugar or less. Shake well with ice, and strain into tulip-shaped glasses, which may be garnished with a small section of orange.

If the chutney is in large pieces, divide them up before bringing to the table.

4 SERVING THE DINNER

Serve whiskey sours.

Serve soup. Arrange deviled crackers on a plate to accompany soup and main course.

For the main course, serve Polynesian shrimp, rice pilaf, and orange-avocado salad sprinkled with 2–3 tbsp. Tahitian dressing. Offer the chutney or Chinese sweet-and-sour sauce as dip for the shrimp.

Pour the wine.

Dessert: sherbet accompanied by fortune cookies or wafers.

DINNER NUMBER 11
SERVES FOUR

SUPPLY CHECKLIST
Check your supply shelf for the following; if missing any item, add to marketing list:

Flour
Nutmeg
Garlic
Black pepper
Lemon

And note, please, that you need a chafing dish or fondue pot with its own Sterno or butane heater to serve the fondue. You should also have four long-handled fondue forks.

MARKETING LIST
1 lb. Gruyère or Emmenthaler cheese (buy 1 solid piece natural cheese—not sliced, packaged, or processed)
$\frac{1}{4}$ lb. thinly sliced Genoa salami
$\frac{1}{4}$ lb. prosciutto or Westphalian ham
Assortment of fresh fruit, such as apples, pears, plums, cherries, melon, or tangerines, whatever is in season
2 long, thin loaves French bread
1 small fruitcake, dark
1 jar sweet midget gherkins
2 bottles Fendant or Neuchâtel (Swiss) or California Sémillon or Riesling
1 bottle (or $\frac{1}{2}$ bottle) kirsch
1 bottle red Dubonnet
1 small jar watermelon pickles

MENU

KIRSCH-DUBONNET COCKTAIL

ROULADES OF SALAMI AND PROSCIUTTO

SWISS CHEESE FONDUE
FRENCH BREAD

FENDANT OR NEUCHÂTEL

FRESH FRUIT PLATTER
FINGERS OF DARK FRUITCAKE

1 PRELIMINARIES

Chill white wine in the refrigerator.

Cut the prosciutto into strips 2 inches wide, and roll into little bundles, securing each with a toothpick. Pull the outer casing off salami slices, and form into small cornucopia rolls, fanning open at one end and pointed at the other. Fasten into shape with toothpicks. Arrange on a platter with mounds of gherkins and watermelon pickles drained of their juices and speared with toothpicks. Chill in refrigerator.

Arrange the fresh fruit platter. Make it a work of art, using a few fresh green lemon leaves under the fruit, and contrasting colors carefully. Tuck three or four small fresh flowers among the fruit, and add, if you like, a few shelled walnuts, dried figs, or glacé fruits for contrast. Keep the platter cool until serving time.

Cut fingers or small wedges of fruitcake—it's easier to slice if first chilled thoroughly in refrigerator. Cover the sliced cake with foil, a cloth, or a pot cover, and put aside to come to room temperature.

2 PREPARING THE MAIN DISH

INGREDIENTS:

1 lb. cheese, Gruyère or Emmenthaler, cubed or coarsely grated
2 tbsp. flour
1 clove garlic

2 c. dry white wine
Nutmeg, black pepper
French bread
2 jiggers kirsch

METHOD:

Mix cheese with flour in a bowl or by shaking together in a brown paper bag. Cut the garlic clove across, and rub the cut surface all over the inside of the fondue pot or chafing dish. Pour in the wine, and toss in the garlic. Heat over medium flame until almost boiling (a few bubbles appearing at the edge). Fish out the garlic clove. Add flour-coated cheese, a handful at a time, to the wine, stirring constantly, just until cheese melts. When all the cheese has been added, grate in a little nutmeg and black pepper, and take pot off the flame. Do not overcook, or fondue will get stringy and tough. Final cooking will be done at the dinner table.

French bread should be warmed in foil in the oven at 400° for 10 minutes.

Then cut into bite-size pieces (1½-inch cubes). Each piece *must* have some crust on it; otherwise it will fall apart when it's dunked.

3 SERVING THE DINNER

Make two kirsch-Dubonnet cocktails by shaking well, with ice, 3 jiggers kirsch, 5 jiggers Dubonnet, and the juice of ½ lemon. Serve the salami-prosciutto roulades with the drinks.

For the main course, put the chafing dish or fondue stand on the dinner table, light the flame, and adjust to a low heat. Set the pan of fondue over the heat, stirring until it simmers, and then add the kirsch. Serve a big basket of French bread chunks. Tell each guest to spear a piece of bread on his fork and twirl it around in the bubbling cheese until it's well coated, then eat and enjoy! In the Jura mountains of France and Switzerland they say that if a girl drops her piece of bread into the fondue, everyone kisses her, but if a man loses his bread, he must buy another bottle of wine for the company. Whatever the rules and the forfeits are, it's a great dish for a party, and the most delicious bite of all is the golden-brown crust left at the bottom of the pan. This tidbit should be scooped out and divided among all the guests.

Pour the wine, replenishing as necessary. Fondue makes you thirsty!

After the fondue is finished, serve the fresh fruit and cake, and perhaps cups of espresso.

DINNER NUMBER 12
SERVES TWO

SUPPLY CHECKLIST
Check your supply shelf for the following; if missing any item, add to marketing list:

Eggs (2)
Butter
Olive oil
Wine vinegar
Salt, pepper
Gin
Tonic water

MARKETING LIST
1 head romaine or leaf lettuce
4 medium-size tomatoes
$\frac{1}{2}$ lb. fresh green beans or 1 medium-
     size can or 1 package frozen
     beans
1 lb. small new potatoes or 1 can
1 green pepper
1–2 fresh limes
1 large, mild onion, Bermuda or red
1 can anchovy fillets
1 $7\frac{1}{2}$-oz. can chunk-style tuna in
     water
1 jar or can black olives, pitted
1 can onion soup
1 tin grated Parmesan cheese
1 small can crushed pineapple in
     natural juice
1 long, thin loaf French bread
1 cheesecake (frozen)
1 bottle Vinho Verde, or Mateus rosé
     (Portugal) or other rosé wine,
     or California Chablis

MENU

GIN AND TONIC

FRENCH ONION SOUP

SALADE NIÇOISE
FRENCH BREAD

VINHO VERDE

CHEESECAKE

1 PRELIMINARIES

Put the wine in the refrigerator to chill. Take cheesecake out to thaw.

Prepare cheese croutons for the soup. Cut 2 ¾-inch slices of the French bread, spread them thinly with butter, and sprinkle with grated cheese. Put under the broiler for 2 or 3 minutes until crisp and brown.

Mix classic French dressing, using 6 tbsp. olive oil, 2 tbsp. wine vinegar, ½ tsp. salt, and a sprinkling of black pepper. Shake together in a screw-top jar and chill.

2 PREPARING THE MAIN DISH

INGREDIENTS:

1 c. whole green beans
6–8 small potatoes, sliced
1 head romaine or leaf lettuce
4 medium-size tomatoes, quartered
2 hard-boiled eggs, quartered
1 mild onion, sliced thin

1 green pepper, sliced thin
8 anchovy fillets, drained and cut in
    small pieces
12 black olives, pitted
1 7½-oz. can tuna, drained and separated
    into chunks

METHOD:

If you are using fresh or frozen green beans and potatoes, cook them, separately, in boiling salted water until just tender. Peel and slice the potatoes after cooking— they will stay firmer and retain the vitamins better. Drain water off, and chill the vegetables. Wash and dry the lettuce leaves, and spread them over a large shallow bowl or platter.

Sprinkle 1–2 tbsp. French dressing over the potatoes and the beans; then arrange all ingredients in rows or mounds on top of the lettuce. Contrast colors and textures artfully. Chill in the refrigerator.

Crisp the French bread wrapped in foil in a 400° oven for 10 minutes.

3 SERVING THE DINNER

To 2 oz. gin in each tall glass, add ice cubes to the top, and fill with tonic.

Make a small slit on the inner side of 2 lime wedges, and perch one on the edge of each glass, so that you can squeeze the lime juice into your drink if you wish.

Heat the onion soup. You may substitute a cold soup, such as jellied consommé or madrilene. Most gourmets, however, agree that even in midsummer weather, an all-cold meal is less inviting, less stimulating to the appetite, than one in which hot and cold dishes provide variety and contrast.

Put a cheese crouton in each soup bowl or cup, and pour the boiling soup over them. Serve a small bowl of grated cheese to stir into the soup at table.

Present the salade Niçoise for the admiration of your guest; then pour over it the rest of the salad dressing from a small pitcher, toss thoroughly, and serve, accompanied by French bread and sweet butter.

Pour the white or rosé wine.

Dessert: cheesecake; add crushed pineapple on top.

DINNER NUMBER 13
SERVES TWO

MENU

MANHATTAN

RELISH PLATTER

BEEF GRANATINE
BAKED POTATOES, GREEN PEAS
PARTY RYE BREAD

BURGUNDY

APPLE TURNOVERS

1 PRELIMINARIES

Prepare the relish platter. Wash and trim radishes, leaving 1 or 2 small leaves on. Take off outside stalks of celery, wash remaining stalks (hearts), and divide in half, or into quarters if very large. Wash and trim green onions, and cut off part of long green stems. Make the yogurt relish as follows: Crush 1 clove of garlic, in a garlic press if you have one. Add $\frac{1}{4}$ tsp. salt, and stir into 1 c. plain yogurt. Peel cucumber, remove any large seeds, and dice it. Add to yogurt-garlic mixture, and stir to mix. Arrange radishes, celery, green onions, olive salad, and yogurt mixture in a lazy Susan, or in five small bowls set on a tray or platter. Chill in refrigerator.

Preheat oven to 400°. Scrub potatoes, and put them in oven to bake. At 400°, they will take 40–50 minutes, but you can speed up either by boiling them for 5 minutes before baking, or by pushing a small metal skewer through each before baking; then bake at least 30 minutes.

When the potatoes are about half done, bake the apple turnovers according to package directions.

Uncork the wine about an hour before dinner.

2 PREPARING THE MAIN DISH

INGREDIENTS:

1 slice white bread
$\frac{3}{4}$ lb. ground chuck
2 eggs
$\frac{1}{4}$ tsp. salt
$\frac{1}{8}$ tsp. pepper
$\frac{1}{8}$ tsp. nutmeg
1 tbsp. Parmesan cheese

Flour
Dry bread crumbs
2 tbsp. butter
1 can tomato sauce
1 small can mushrooms, for sauce
Thyme or oregano

METHOD:

Soak the bread in water; squeeze dry. Mix ground chuck, bread, one egg, seasonings, and cheese. This is easiest to do with your hands, but remember to take off rings first. Form into four even portions, and flatten into ovals about $\frac{1}{2}$ inch thick. Dip first in flour, then in a beaten egg, and then in bread crumbs, pressing each patty so it is evenly coated. Melt butter in frying pan, and cook the patties over medium heat until golden brown, about 3 minutes on each side. Remove from pan and keep them warm.

Add $\frac{1}{4}$ c. water to the frying pan, and mix with brown fat and drippings. Add tomato sauce and mushrooms, and simmer for a few minutes, adding a little salt and pepper to taste and a pinch of thyme or oregano.

While sauce simmers, cook the frozen peas and onions according to package directions.

3 SERVING THE DINNER

Chill the cocktail glasses. Make two Manhattans with 2 jiggers rye whiskey and $\frac{1}{2}$ jigger each sweet and dry vermouth. Stir well with ice, and strain into glasses, on the rocks or straight up. Add a twist of lemon peel to each cocktail. Put relish platter on the dining table.

For the main course, serve the beef granatine on warmed plates with the tomato-mushroom sauce poured over. Slit baked potatoes on top to tuck in a generous pat of butter and serve along with peas.

Arrange slices of party rye bread in a small basket. Pour the wine.

Dessert: hot apple turnovers sprinkled with a little powdered sugar.

DINNER NUMBER 14
SERVES FOUR

SUPPLY CHECKLIST
Check your supply shelf for the following; if missing any item, add to marketing list:
Butter
Garlic
Dried tarragon
Salt, pepper
Vodka

MARKETING LIST
2 lbs. *lean* lamb, ground
1 lb. onions
2 small cucumbers
1 head lettuce, chicory, escarole, or
    1 bunch watercress
1 bunch parsley
4 lemons
2 packages frozen French fried
    potatoes
1 8-oz. carton sour cream
1 pound cake
1 loaf Italian bread
1 pint coffee ice cream
1 3-oz. jar red (salmon) caviar
1 large can tomatoes
1 bottle Italian dressing
2 bottles red wine, Burgundy or
    Rhône
1 small bottle Kahlúa or other liqueur

MENU

VODKA

CUCUMBERS

LAMB ESPAGNOL
FRENCH FRIED POTATOES, GREEN SALAD
GARLIC BREAD

RED BURGUNDY

POUND CAKE

1 PRELIMINARIES

Prepare appetizer: Peel cucumbers. Split them lengthwise, and hollow out seeds and pulp to make four boat-shaped portions. Marinate in the refrigerator with 3 or 4 tbsp. Italian dressing for ½ hour. Mix the salmon caviar with ½ c. sour cream and chill in the refrigerator until serving.

Wash and drain salad greens, and tear them in pieces. Put in salad bowl, and refrigerate.

Uncork the wine about an hour before dinner.

2 PREPARING THE MAIN DISH

INGREDIENTS:

- 2 lbs. ground lamb
- 1 onion, chopped
- 1 clove garlic, minced
- ¼ c. fresh parsley, chopped
- ½ tsp. salt
- ¼ tsp. pepper
- 2 tbsp. butter
- 2 c. canned tomatoes
- ½ c. lemon juice

METHOD:

Mix lamb, onion, garlic, parsley, salt, and pepper. Spread mixture 1 inch thick in a buttered baking dish. Dot with small pieces of butter; bake for 30 minutes in a 350° oven. Spread canned tomatoes over the top of the meat, dividing any large pieces of tomato. Bake another 30 minutes.

Pour the lemon juice over the mixture, and bake 10 minutes more.

While the lamb is cooking, heat and crisp the potatoes according to package directions. Brush Italian bread with garlic-flavored melted butter, wrap in foil, and warm in the oven for 10 minutes.

3 FINAL ASSEMBLY

Drain the cucumbers from their Italian-dressing marinade. Fill the hollowed-out centers with the caviar-sour cream mixture, and garnish with tiny parsley sprigs.

Add 1 tbsp. chopped fresh parsley and a pinch of tarragon to 3–4 tbsp. Italian dressing, and spread over the green salad.

4 SERVING THE DINNER

Put 2 oz. of vodka on the rocks with a wedge of lemon, adding water, soda, or tonic if desired, for each drink.

Serve stuffed cucumber appetizer on individual plates.

For the main course, serve lamb Espagnol cut into squares, along with French fried potatoes. Accompany with green salad and garlic bread.

Pour the wine.

Dessert: slices of pound cake topped with a scoop of ice cream, over which you pour 1 or 2 tsp. Kahlúa. If you don't have Kahlúa, use another liqueur such as Drambuie or Grand Marnier, but sprinkle those over the cake before adding the ice cream. Rum, sherry, or brandy may be used in this way, too, to give a fillip to the cake.

DINNER NUMBER 15
SERVES TWO

SUPPLY CHECKLIST
Check your supply shelf for the following; if missing any item, add to marketing list:

Milk
Egg (1)
Butter
Flour
Garlic
Soy sauce
Ground ginger
Prepared mustard
Salt, pepper
Heavy-duty aluminum foil
Light rum
Bottled salad dressing

MARKETING LIST
1 large chicken breast
1 large ripe avocado
1 or 2 thin-skinned oranges
1 lb. fresh spinach
1 lb. onions
1 small package sliced American cheese
1 can mushroom caps or $\frac{1}{4}$ lb. fresh mushrooms
1 package rice (white, long grain)
1 package shredded coconut
1 can pineapple juice
1 small loaf white sandwich bread
1 or 2 packages breadsticks, sesame and salted
1 pint vanilla ice cream
1 bottle Muscadet
1 small bottle grenadine (syrup or liqueur) or other liqueur

MENU

PINEAPPLE-RUM COCKTAIL

TOASTED CHEESE TIDBITS

CHICKEN LUAU
BUTTERED RICE, ORANGE-AVOCADO SALAD
ASSORTED BREADSTICKS

MUSCADET

VANILLA ICE CREAM

1 PRELIMINARIES

Put wine in refrigerator to chill.

Prepare the toasted cheese tidbits: Spread 2 slices of bread with butter, 2 with prepared mustard. Lay 2 thin slices of American cheese on each of the buttered bread slices, and top each slice with another piece of bread, mustard side in. Press firmly together, and cut off crusts with a sharp knife. Set aside.

Prepare the salad: Peel the oranges, taking off all the piths as well as the yellow skins. Slice in $\frac{1}{2}$-inch-thick rings. Peel and section the avocado. Arrange alternating slices of orange and avocado on a platter or in a shallow bowl. Drizzle a little juice from the end slices of orange over the avocado to prevent discoloration. Chill in the refrigerator.

2 PREPARING THE MAIN DISH

INGREDIENTS:

1 large chicken breast	$\frac{1}{4}$ c. dry white wine
1–2 tbsp. flour	2 tsp. soy sauce
3 tbsp. butter	4 mushroom caps, sliced
1 lb. fresh spinach, carefully washed	Salt, pepper, ground ginger
$\frac{1}{2}$ small onion, minced	2 12-inch squares of heavy aluminum foil
1 small garlic clove, minced	

METHOD:

Divide chicken breast lengthwise to make two even pieces. Make sure pieces are well trimmed, i.e., wings removed, ends of rib bones cut short, and skin taken off. Dip lightly in flour. Melt butter in skillet, and fry chicken pieces on both sides until golden brown. Arrange 6 or 8 large spinach leaves on each square of foil; place chicken breast on top of the spinach. Mix together: onion, garlic, wine, soy sauce, and mushrooms, and spread half over each piece of chicken. Season with salt, pepper, and ginger. Cover each portion with 3 or 4 more spinach leaves. Bring up two sides of foil evenly, and make a double fold to seal them together. Then seal the ends firmly enough to keep in all the juices. Put the chicken pieces on a flat baking tin, and keep them in the oven at a moderate heat (350°) for 1 hour.

While the chicken is cooking, prepare the rice according to package directions. When rice is cooked, fluff with a fork, and add 1–2 tbsp. of butter.

3 FINAL ASSEMBLY

Mix the pineapple-rum cocktail: Shake well with ice 2 jiggers light rum, 2 jiggers pineapple juice, and 2 tsp. grenadine. Strain into chilled glasses.

Sprinkle the salad with 2–3 tbsp. bottled dressing, or make your own dressing of 2 tbsp. oil, 1 tbsp. lemon juice, and a dash of salt and pepper.

4 SERVING THE DINNER

Serve drinks, accompanied by hot cheese tidbits.

For the main course, bring chicken luau to the table right in its foil package— just open the seal and fold back the edges —accompanied by buttered rice on plates.

Put $\frac{1}{4}$ c. coconut on a flat tin to toast in the 350° oven for a few minutes.

Beat 1 egg with $\frac{1}{4}$ c. milk. Dip the cheese sandwiches in the mixture and drain. Melt 3 tbsp. butter in a skillet, and fry sandwiches over gentle heat until golden brown on both sides. Cut in small squares or triangles, and serve hot, on a folded paper napkin, with the pineapple-rum cocktails.

Serve salad and breadsticks.

Pour the white wine.

Dessert: vanilla ice cream in dessert dishes, topped with 1 tsp. grenadine, Kahlúa, or other liqueur and a sprinkle of toasted coconut.

DINNER NUMBER 16
SERVES TWO

SUPPLY CHECKLIST
Check your supply shelf for the following; if missing any item, add to marketing list:

Oil
Wine vinegar
Garlic
Salt, pepper
Worcestershire sauce
Small skewers (4)
Powdered sugar
Lemon

MARKETING LIST
1 flank steak
$\frac{1}{2}$ lb. sliced bacon
1 bunch green onions
1 bunch parsley
1 large mild onion
1 small head lettuce
1 can whole green beans or $\frac{1}{2}$ lb. fresh beans
1 can whole baby beets
1 package noodles Romanoff
1 jar herring fillets in cream sauce
1 package bake-and-serve hard rolls
1 bottle or package instant meat-tenderizer
1 package bake-and-serve apple turnovers
1 bottle Dubonnet blonde
1 bottle French red Bordeaux or California Cabernet or Zinfandel

MENU

DUBONNET BLONDE

HERRING FILLETS

BEEF ROULADES
NOODLES ROMANOFF, BABY BEETS
AND GREEN BEANS VINAIGRETTE
SMALL HARD ROLLS

FRENCH RED BORDEAUX

BAKED FRUIT TURNOVERS

1 PRELIMINARIES

Wash, drain, and dry the lettuce. Drain the canned beets and arrange in the middle of a salad platter or shallow bowl. Arrange the drained canned green beans around them. If using fresh green beans, first cook, drain, and cool them. Cut 3 or 4 paper-thin slices of the large onion, separate into rings, and scatter on top of beets and beans. Decorate if desired with a few of the little inside leaves from the lettuce. Cover the bowl with plastic wrap and refrigerate it.

Line two small plates with the larger lettuce leaves, and arrange herring in cream sauce over them. Chill in the refrigerator.

Make vinaigrette sauce by shaking together in a screw-top jar 3 tbsp. oil, 1 tbsp. vinegar, $\frac{1}{2}$ tsp. salt, and a dash of pepper. Add a few drops of Worcestershire sauce and 1 tbsp. finely chopped parsley.

Uncork the wine about an hour before dinner.

2 PREPARING THE MAIN DISH

INGREDIENTS:

1 flank steak	**2 tbsp. parsley, chopped**
Instant meat-tenderizer	**Salt, pepper**
2 tbsp. green onions, chopped	**4 slices bacon**
1 clove garlic, chopped	**4 small skewers**

METHOD:

Flatten flank steak a little by pounding it. There is a special hammer-like object designed for this job, but if you don't own one, you can get the same result with a rolling pin or even an empty soda bottle. The idea is to get the meat an even thickness all over and to make it more or less rectangular. However, if there are straggly edges, just trim them off and lay them on top of the large piece. Sprinkle the meat with tenderizer according to package directions. Then spread with the onions, garlic, parsley, salt, and pepper. Roll the meat up like a jelly roll, starting with the long edge. Cut the rolled steak into four even portions. Wrap a slice of bacon around each roll, and fasten securely in place with a small skewer.

Preheat oven, and cook noodles Romanoff according to package directions. Bake apple turnovers at the same time. When both are done, remove them from oven, turn up heat to broil, and cook the beef rolls, 3 inches below the flame, for about 5 minutes. Turn and cook on second side for 4 minutes more; if well-done steaks are desired, increase cooking time by 1–2 minutes for each side.

3 SERVING THE DINNER

Pour Dubonnet over ice cubes in old-fashioned glasses, with a twist of lemon. Serve herring appetizers.

For the main course, serve beef roulades and noodles Romanoff on warmed plates. Shake vinaigrette dressing, and pour over beets and green beans; stir at table.

Pour the wine.

Dessert: apple turnovers lightly sprinkled with powdered sugar.

DINNER NUMBER 17
SERVES TWO

SUPPLY CHECKLIST
Check your supply shelf for the following; if missing any item, add to marketing list:

Olive oil
Tabasco
Wine vinegar
Garlic
Bottled capers
Egg (1)
Crème de cassis (French black currant liqueur)
Salt, pepper
Butter

MARKETING LIST:
2 frozen lobster tails
1 package frozen asparagus or 1 lb. fresh asparagus
1 package frozen raspberries
1 package frozen potato puffs
1 can consommé madrilene
1 loaf French bread
1 small angel food cake
½ pint heavy cream or 1 dispenser ready-whipped cream
1 bottle Chenin Blanc or other medium-dry white wine

MENU

KIR

JELLIED MADRILENE

BROILED ROCK LOBSTER TAILS
POTATO PUFFS, COLD ASPARAGUS SALAD
FRENCH BREAD

CHENIN BLANC

ANGEL FOOD CAKE

1 PRELIMINARIES

Chill canned madrilene and wine overnight. Evening of dinner, take raspberries out of refrigerator to thaw. Cook frozen or fresh asparagus till just tender; drain and chill. Hard-boil 1 egg (put in cold water, bring to boil, simmer 10 minutes), and run cold water over it. Make French dressing with 3 tbsp. oil, 1 tbsp. wine vinegar, $\frac{1}{2}$ tsp. salt, and a dash of pepper. Shake in a screw-top jar and chill.

2 PREPARING THE MAIN DISH

INGREDIENTS:

2 lobster tails	**4 drops Tabasco**
$\frac{1}{4}$ lb. butter	**1 small clove garlic, crushed**

METHOD:

Preheat oven to temperature given on package of potato puffs.

With a heavy sharp knife, cut through the hard upper shell of the lobster tail, opening it butterfly style, without cutting through the thin undershell. Melt butter; add Tabasco and crushed garlic, and brush over the cut surfaces of the lobster. (The remaining butter may be used as a sauce to pour over the lobsters at the dinner table.)

Heat potato puffs according to package directions.

Turn oven up to broil. Give it about 5 minutes to heat; meanwhile, put the potato puffs in foil on top of stove to keep them warm. Broil lobster 4–5 inches from heat, for 8–9 minutes. When lobster tails are cooked, turn oven heat down to lowest setting, open the oven door, and put lobster and potato puffs in there to keep hot until serving time without overcooking.

3 FINAL ASSEMBLY

Arrange asparagus spears on two salad plates. Shake the French dressing, and pour half over each portion. Sprinkle with the hard-boiled egg, chopped, and 1 tsp. of chopped capers ($\frac{1}{2}$ tsp. on each plate—capers are quite strongly flavored).

Wrap French bread in foil, and heat in 400° oven for ten minutes.

If using heavy cream for the dessert, whip till stiff.

Mix the Kir as follows: Chill large wineglasses (flutes if you have them—these are tall, narrow wineglasses that the French prefer for champagne and other sparkling wines, similar in shape to a parfait glass).

Put 1 tbsp. crème de cassis in each glass, and fill ⅔ full with icy cold white wine; stir. Vin blanc cassis has been a tradition for festive occasions in the city of Dijon for at least fifty years, but was renamed Kir in honor of a much-admired wartime mayor of the city.

4 SERVING THE DINNER

Serve the Kir cocktail.

Spoon jellied madrilene into cups and add lemon section to each.

For the main course, serve broiled lobster tails and potato puffs on warmed plates. Use the rest of the hot melted butter as sauce. Serve the asparagus salad. Put slices of French bread in a basket. Pour the wine.

Dessert: slices of angel food cake topped with thawed raspberries and whipped cream.

DINNER NUMBER 18
SERVES FOUR

SUPPLY CHECKLIST
Check your supply shelf for the following; if missing any items, add them to marketing list:

Butter
Peanut oil
Wine vinegar
Soy sauce
Garlic
Lemon (1)
Egg (1)
Salt, pepper
Orange bitters
Superfine sugar

MARKETING LIST
1½–2 lbs. sole fillets (4 large or 8 small)
1 cucumber
1 bunch green onions
1 lb. tomatoes
1 fresh ginger root or powdered ginger
2 packages French-cut green beans
1 package rice (white, long-grain)
1 package Saltines or plain crackers
1 package frozen egg rolls
Almond cookies
Fortune cookies
2 cans black bean soup
1 bottle medium-dry sherry
2 bottles dry Sauterne or Chablis wine
Almonds

MENU

SHERRY AND BITTERS

BLACK BEAN SOUP

FISH MALAYAN
GREEN BEANS WITH ALMONDS
BUTTERED RICE
EGG ROLLS
SLICED TOMATO AND CUCUMBER

DRY SAUTERNE

ALMOND COOKIES

1 PRELIMINARIES

Chill the wine.

Peel and slice cucumber. Slice tomatoes, and arrange on platter in alternate rows. Chop one of the green onions, and scatter over the top. Chill in refrigerator. Make a simple French dressing with 3 tbsp. oil and 1 tbsp. wine vinegar. Shake in a small screw-top jar with $\frac{1}{2}$ tsp. salt, $\frac{1}{2}$ tsp. superfine sugar, and a dash of pepper. Chill the dressing. Hard-boil 1 egg (put in cold water, bring to boil, simmer 10 minutes); cool under cold running water.

2 PREPARING THE MAIN DISH

INGREDIENTS:

- **1 bunch green onions**
- **1 clove garlic**
- **1–2 lbs. sole fillets**
- **$\frac{1}{4}$ c. peanut oil**
- **4 tbsp. soy sauce**
- **$\frac{1}{4}$ c. sherry**
- **1 tbsp. grated or very finely chopped fresh ginger. If fresh ginger root is not available, use $\frac{1}{2}$ tsp. powdered ginger.**

METHOD:

Chop onions and garlic, and put in baking dish suitable for the table. Place neatly trimmed fish fillets on top. Combine oil, soy sauce, and sherry, and pour half of mixture over fillets. Sprinkle with ginger. Broil 3 inches from flame for 10 minutes or until fish flakes easily with a fork.

While fish is cooking, prepare rice according to package directions, and heat egg rolls. Cook green beans (they take about 5 minutes). Drain and add $\frac{1}{2}$ c. almonds and 2 tbsp. butter. Toss together. As soon as rice is cooked, fluff with a fork, add 2 tbsp. butter, and cover pan with a clean, dry dish towel. Replace lid (so rice will not get soggy) until ready to serve.

3 FINAL ASSEMBLY

Shake dressing, and pour over tomato-and-cucumber salad.

Heat black bean soup, and add 2 tbsp. sherry, or more if you prefer. At serving time, pour into bowls or soup cups, and garnish each guest's serving with a thin slice of lemon topped with a slice of hard-boiled egg.

4 SERVING THE DINNER

Pour sherry over crushed ice with 1 or 2 dashes of orange bitters in each glass.

Serve black bean soup along with a small basket of Saltines or plain crackers.

For the main course, bring fish Malayan to the table in its baking dish, accompanied by buttered rice in bowls, green beans, and egg rolls. No bread is necessary with this menu.

Pour Sauterne or Chablis.

Dessert: fortune cookies and almond cookies; a cup of jasmine tea would be a delicious accompaniment.

DINNER NUMBER 19
SERVES FOUR

SUPPLY CHECKLIST
Check your supply shelf for the following; if missing any item, add to marketing list:

Chicken bouillon cube
Butter
Oil
Flour
Garlic
Salt, pepper, paprika, garlic powder
Lemon
Basil, dry or fresh
Sweet vermouth
Club soda

MARKETING LIST
4 small veal shanks, cut in 3-inch lengths (2 pieces per person)
$\frac{1}{4}$–$\frac{1}{3}$ lb. Cotto or Genoa salami, sliced *very* thin (16 slices)
4 ripe pears (Comice or Anjou)
Lettuce, chicory, and escarole, 1 small head each
1 bunch parsley
1 bunch radishes
1 large package fine noodles
1 loaf Italian bread
1 can artichoke hearts
1 small jar or can red pimento strips
1 can tomato paste
1 ripe Camembert cheese, French or American (preferably fresh from a cheese store, not from supermarket dairy case)
1 box plain crackers or wheatmeal biscuits
1 bottle Italian dressing
1 jar olive salad
2 bottles Valpolicella or Bardolino or a similar American dry red wine

MENU

SWEET VERMOUTH

COTTO SALAMI

OSSO BUCO
BUTTERED NOODLES
GREEN SALAD, GARLIC BREAD

VALPOLICELLA

FRESH PEARS AND CAMEMBERT

1 PRELIMINARIES

Wash, drain, and dry salad greens. Wrap in a clean towel or paper towel, and store in the refrigerator. An hour before serving, tear salad greens into pieces, and put in a large salad bowl. Garnish with drained artichoke hearts and pimento strips. Refrigerate until serving time.

Uncork the wine an hour early.

2 PREPARING THE MAIN DISH

INGREDIENTS:

4 **veal shanks**	$\frac{1}{3}$ **c. (5 tbsp.) tomato paste**
$\frac{1}{4}$ **c. flour**	1 **c. white wine**
$\frac{1}{2}$ **tsp. salt**	2 **cloves crushed garlic**
$\frac{1}{4}$ **tsp. pepper**	1 **strip lemon peel**
$\frac{1}{2}$ **tsp. paprika**	1 **tsp. basil**
$\frac{1}{4}$ **c. oil**	

METHOD:

Mix flour, salt, pepper, and paprika in a paper bag. Shake veal shanks in the bag to coat them all over.

Heat oil in casserole, and brown meat thoroughly on all sides. Add all other ingredients. Cover and simmer gently $1\frac{1}{2}$ hours until meat is very tender. Turn meat over twice, and add a little more broth (make it with a chicken bouillon cube), if necessary. When shanks are fork-tender, remove them from pan. Cook sauce for a few minutes to thicken slightly, and put meat back in the sauce to keep hot.

While the veal shanks are cooking, cook the noodles. Drain and toss with butter.

Prepare the garlic bread by slashing bread at 2-inch intervals without cutting through the bottom crust. Brush melted butter seasoned with garlic powder between slices and on top. Heat until crisp in a 300° oven, wrapped in foil.

3 FINAL ASSEMBLY

Arrange the slices of salami on small plates. Wash the radishes, leaving a small sprig of leaves if possible. Garnish each serving of salami with 3 or 4 radishes cut into pretty shapes and a small mound of olive salad.

4 SERVING THE DINNER

Pour 2 jiggers sweet vermouth over ice cubes in wineglasses or large cocktail glasses. Add a twist of lemon peel and a little club soda. Serve salami with radishes and olive salad.

For the main course, serve osso buco sprinkled with chopped parsley, along with noodles, on warmed plates. Pour 2–3 tbsp. Italian dressing over the salad, and toss when you bring it to the table. Pour the wine.

Dessert: Slice pears, and cut Camembert into wedges. Offer them with a platter or basket of crackers. The cheese should be kept at room temperature for at least 1 hour before serving so that it is soft and creamy. Each guest should have a dessert plate.

DINNER NUMBER 20
SERVES TWO

SUPPLY CHECKLIST
Check your supply shelf for the following; if missing any item, add to marketing list:

Rice (white, long grain)
Butter
Garlic
Tabasco
Dried tarragon
French dressing
Grenadine
Ready-blended herb seasoning

MARKETING LIST
2 lamb steaks, $\frac{3}{4}$–1 inch thick
1 bunch carrots
1 bunch celery
1 package frozen broccoli or 1 bunch fresh broccoli
1 large lime or 2 small
1 lb. tomatoes
1 can large green olives
$\frac{1}{4}$ lb. Greek black olives in oil
1 package bake-and-serve small hard rolls
1 pint lime sherbet
1 small package Roquefort or other blue cheese
1 bottle red Chianti or Vino de Tavola
1 bottle (fifth or pint) Puerto Rican rum, light
1 small bottle Cointreau or other fruit-flavored liqueur

MENU

BACARDI COCKTAIL

RAW CARROT AND CELERY STICKS
BLACK AND GREEN OLIVES

SAVORY LAMB STEAKS
BROCCOLI, HERB-FLAVORED RICE
SLICED TOMATOES WITH TARRAGON
HARD ROLLS AND BUTTER

RED CHIANTI

LIME SHERBET

1 PRELIMINARIES

Wash and scrape or peel carrots, and cut into sticks. Wash celery very carefully, pull off outer stalks (use them for soup or stew another day), and cut the tender inner parts lengthwise into 4 pieces. Crisp carrots and celery in a glass of cold water in the refrigerator.

Slice tomatoes, and arrange on a platter or in a shallow bowl. Sprinkle lightly with tarragon.

Uncork the wine about an hour before dinner.

2 PREPARING THE MAIN DISH

INGREDIENTS:

2 oz. Roquefort or other blue cheese	**2 dashes Tabasco**
1 small garlic clove, crushed	**2 lamb steaks**

METHOD:

Cook ⅔ c. rice according to package directions. When cooked, add 2 tbsp. butter and a pinch of ready-blended herb seasoning to taste. Keep warm until served.

Set oven to broil. Mash the blue cheese to a paste, blending in the garlic and Tabasco. Using half the paste, spread one side of each steak. Broil 5 minutes, 3 inches from broiler flame. Turn the steaks over, and spread them with the remaining cheese paste. Broil 3 or 4 minutes more, until the steaks are cooked through.

Cook broccoli while lamb steaks are under the broiler. Heat hard rolls at the same time.

3 SERVING THE DINNER

Chill glasses. Mix Bacardi cocktail: Shake well with ice 4 jiggers of rum, the juice of 1 large lime, and 1 tbsp. grenadine. Strain into chilled glasses.

Arrange celery and carrot sticks with the black and green olives, and serve them with the drinks.

For the main course, serve lamb steaks, broccoli, and herb-flavored rice on warmed plates. Sprinkle about 3 tbsp.

bottled French dressing over tomato salad. Serve hard rolls with or without butter as desired. Pour the wine.

Dessert: lime sherbet with a little Cointreau or other fruit-flavored liqueur sprinkled on top.

DINNER NUMBER 21
SERVES TWO

Check your supply shelf for the following; if missing any item, add to marketing list:

Oil
Wine vinegar
Butter
Flour
Salt, pepper
Nutmeg
Dried tarragon
Sugar (superfine granulated)
Powdered sugar

MARKETING LIST
2 whole chicken breasts, split in half
(without wings)
$\frac{1}{4}$ lb. prosciutto or thinly sliced
boiled ham
1 large bunch fresh spinach, 1–1$\frac{1}{2}$ lbs.
1 large lime
1 ripe cantaloupe
1 lb. small new potatoes
1 8-oz. carton sour cream
1 small can seedless white grapes
1 package frozen raspberry turnovers
1 package breadsticks
1 bottle Sauvignon Blanc or Lieb-
fraumilch
1 bottle (fifth or pint) white rum,
Puerto Rican or Virgin Island

MENU

DAIQUIRI

MELON

CHICKEN VERONICA
BUTTERED NEW POTATOES
SPINACH SALAD
BREADSTICKS

SAUVIGNON BLANC

RASPBERRY TURNOVERS

1 PRELIMINARIES

Chill wine in refrigerator.

Cut 4 narrow lengthwise slices of cantaloupe. Remove rind and wind strips of prosciutto ham around each slice. Cover with plastic wrap or foil, and chill.

Scrub new potatoes, and cook in boiling salted water until just tender. Drain and cool about 15–20 minutes so they can be handled. They will be easier to peel *and* more nutritious if peeled *after* cooking.

Wash the spinach, and pick out the small, tender light green leaves for the salad. (Save the rest of it for another meal.) Put 2 tbsp. oil, 1 tbsp. vinegar, $\frac{1}{2}$ tsp. salt, and a dash of pepper into a small bowl. Beat with a fork or whisk. Add 4 tbsp. sour cream, and $\frac{1}{2}$ tsp. sugar if desired. Beat until blended and smooth. Chill.

2 PREPARING THE MAIN DISH

INGREDIENTS:

2 chicken breasts, split in half (4 pieces)
1 c. dry white wine
Pinch of tarragon
2 tbsp. butter
2 tbsp. flour
Salt, pepper, nutmeg
Small can seedless white grapes, drained of juices

METHOD:

In a covered skillet, gently simmer the chicken breasts in the wine and tarragon until tender, about $\frac{1}{2}$ hour. Turn breasts over once during cooking; if the wine has reduced, add a few tbsp. water. When breasts are tender, remove from liquid, and put them on a warmed serving platter covered with foil while you make the sauce. Melt 2 tbsp. butter in small pan, and stir in 2 tbsp. flour. Remove from heat. Measure the liquid in which the chicken breasts were cooked. If necessary, add water to make 1 c. Stir gradually into flour-butter mixture, keeping smooth and free from lumps. Put back on moderate heat, and stir with a small whisk until mixture boils and thickens. Add salt, pepper, and nutmeg to taste. Then add well-drained grapes.

While chicken is cooking, bake raspberry turnovers. When they are ready, turn oven to low (250°), and put the chicken in the oven to keep warm until serving time.

3 FINAL ASSEMBLY

Peel the potatoes (the skins will rub off easily), and reheat over a very low flame with 2 tbsp. butter and 1 tbsp. water. Don't let them fry; just steam gently until hot.

4 SERVING THE DINNER

Chill glasses. Put 3 jiggers rum, the juice of 1 large lime, and 1 tbsp. superfine sugar in a shaker with ice. Shake well, and strain into chilled glasses. This is even better if made in a blender with crushed or shaved ice. Sugar may be increased or decreased to taste. Serve melon-prosciutto slices with cocktails, or as first course.

For the main course, serve chicken breasts with sauce poured over them on serving platter. Surround with the new potatoes. Pour sour cream dressing over spinach in the salad bowl, and toss to blend at the table. Serve breadsticks. Pour the wine.

Dessert: raspberry turnovers with a sprinkling of powdered sugar over them.

DINNER NUMBER 22
SERVES TWO

SUPPLY CHECKLIST
Check your supply shelf for the following; if missing any item, add to marketing list:

Butter
Eggs (2)
Milk
Mayonnaise
Garlic powder
Dry ginger
Chili sauce
Bottled capers
Gin
Curry powder
Salt

MARKETING LIST
1 lb. shrimp; largest size 8–12 per lb.
1 lime
1 head romaine lettuce
1 large ripe avocado
2 large tomatoes
2 ripe pears or 1 can large pear halves
1 small can extra-large colossal-size
        black olives
1 small can chocolate sauce
1 can cream of chicken soup
1 loaf French bread
1 pint vanilla ice cream
Quinine water (tonic)
1 bottle Alsatian or domestic Riesling
        (dry white wine)

MENU

GIN AND TONIC

SENEGALESE SOUP

SHRIMP-AVOCADO LOUISE
GARLIC BREAD

RIESLING

PEARS

1 PRELIMINARIES

Chill wine in refrigerator.

Hard-boil 2 eggs: Put them in cold water with 2 tbsp. salt. Bring to a boil, and simmer for 10 minutes. Cool under running water. Take off outside leaves of romaine and discard them. Choose 4 large perfect leaves, wash them, drain, and pat dry with paper towels. Chill them in refrigerator (use rest of romaine another day).

Melt 1 tbsp. butter in a saucepan. Stir in 1 tsp. curry powder and $\frac{1}{4}$ tsp. dry ginger, smoothing out any undissolved lumps. Add cream of chicken soup and 1 c. milk. Simmer 5 minutes to blend flavors.

2 PREPARING THE MAIN DISH

INGREDIENTS:

2 large tomatoes, peeled and quartered
4 large leaves romaine
1 lb. shrimps, largest size or at least 6 shrimps for each serving
1 avocado
$\frac{1}{2}$ c. mayonnaise

$\frac{1}{2}$ c. chili sauce
1 tsp. capers, drained
2 hard-boiled eggs, quartered
1 small can extra-large colossal-size black olives

METHOD:

Skin the tomatoes by dipping them for a few seconds (count up to ten) in rapidly boiling water. Take them out of pan, and cool them under running water. The skins will peel off very easily. Chill.

Shell and devein the shrimp. Simmer 5–6 minutes in boiling water with 1 tbsp. salt added. Drain and cool.

Line two plates with the romaine leaves. Cut shrimp in half lengthwise, and arrange in rows on the romaine. Cut the avocado in half lengthwise. Remove seed, peel the halves, and cut in crosswise slices.

Arrange the avocado slices alternating with the shrimp. Mix mayonnaise, chili sauce, and capers, and spoon over rows of shrimp and avocado. Garnish plates attractively with black olives and quarters of tomato and hard-boiled egg. Chill in the refrigerator till serving time.

Slash the French bread at intervals, without cutting through the bottom crust. Brush with 2 tbsp. melted butter seasoned with garlic powder. Bake, wrapped in foil, in a 350° oven until hot and crisp (approximately 10 minutes).

3 FINAL ASSEMBLY

If using fresh pears, peel them and cut in half lengthwise. With a sharp knife cut out all the core and fibrous section in the middle. Cut off a very tiny slice from the rounded sides so they will sit steadily on the plates and not skid. Refrigerate.

4 SERVING THE DINNER

Fill tall glasses with ice cubes, and put a wedge of lime in each glass. Pour 1½ jiggers gin in each, and fill with tonic (quinine water).

Ladle the hot soup into soup bowls or cups.

For the main course, serve the shrimp-avocado salad accompanied by a basket of garlic bread.

Pour the wine.

Dessert: Put 2 pear halves on each plate. Place a small scoop of ice cream in the hollowed-out core of each half, and top with 1 or 2 spoonfuls of chocolate sauce.

DINNER NUMBER 23
SERVES TWO

Check your supply shelf for the following; if missing any item, add to marketing list:

Olive oil
Butter
Flour
Whole cloves
Salt, pepper
Sweet vermouth

MARKETING LIST
4 veal chops
8–10 thin slices Italian salami, less than $\frac{1}{4}$ lb.
1–2 tomatoes
1 lemon
1 bunch parsley
1 head lettuce or leaf lettuce
1 lb. pearl onions (small white)
1 package frozen Italian-style green beans
1 can artichoke hearts
1 small can green olives
1 small can black olives
1 can rolled anchovy fillets
1 package breadsticks
1 package narrow noodles
1 small package slivered almonds
1 small can or jar pimentos
1 pint spumoni ice cream or biscuit tortoni
1 bottle Orvieto or white Chianti
1 bottle Campari
1 quart club soda

MENU

AMERICANO

ANTIPASTO
BREADSTICKS

VEAL CHOPS MILANO
BUTTERED NOODLES
ITALIAN GREEN BEANS

ORVIETO

SPUMONI

1 PRELIMINARIES

Chill the wine in the refrigerator.

Arrange antipasto platter: Line a flat serving dish with washed and drained lettuce leaves. Arrange on it salami slices, rolled and pinned with toothpicks, anchovy fillets, drained artichoke hearts, pimento halves, and clusters of black and green olives. Garnish with quarters of tomato. Group the ingredients to contrast colors, and fix in place with toothpicks if necessary. Chill in refrigerator until serving time.

2 PREPARING THE MAIN DISH

INGREDIENTS:

4 veal chops	1 pearl onion, peeled and stuck with a
Flour, salt, pepper	whole clove
2 tbsp. butter	1 tsp. chopped parsley
1 tbsp. olive oil	$\frac{1}{2}$ c. dry white wine

METHOD:

Mix flour, salt, and pepper together, and coat chops with the mixture by shaking together in a paper bag. Melt butter with oil in a heavy casserole. Sauté chops over a low flame until golden brown on both sides, about 10 minutes. Add onion and parsley to pan, and pour in wine. Cover pan, and simmer meat gently until tender, about 45 minutes.

While veal is cooking, boil noodles until just tender in salted water with 1 tbsp. oil added (this prevents sticking together). Drain; add 1 tbsp. butter, and stir.

Cook Italian-style green beans according to package directions. Heat 2 tbsp. slivered almonds with 2 tbsp. melted butter. When beans are cooked and drained, stir in the almonds and the butter.

3 SERVING THE DINNER

Make the Americano as follows: Fill 2 tall glasses with ice cubes, pour 2 jiggers sweet vermouth and 1 jigger Campari in each. Fill with club soda, and add a twist of lemon peel. Serve the antipasto platter along with a basket of breadsticks.

For the main course, serve the veal chops Milano with buttered noodles and green beans with almonds. Pour the Orvieto or Chianti.

Dessert: spumoni or biscuit tortoni on small dishes.

DINNER NUMBER 24
SERVES TWO

SUPPLY CHECKLIST
Check your supply shelf for the following; if missing any item, add to marketing list:
Egg (1)
Butter
Powdered sugar
Soy sauce
Garlic
Salt, pepper
Whole nutmeg

MARKETING LIST
1 small frying chicken, cut in pieces
1 bunch parsley
1 head lettuce
1 package frozen Chinese pea pods (snow peas)
1 ripe fresh pineapple
1 lemon
1 jar marinated mushrooms
1 can tiny shrimps
1 package rice (white, long grain)
1 package melba toast
1 box fortune cookies or plain sugar cookies
1 jar strained honey
1 bottle sake
1 bottle dry Sauterne
1 small bottle Cointreau or other liqueur

MENU

SAKE

POTTED SHRIMP

KOREAN CHICKEN
PARSLEY RICE, CHINESE PEA PODS
GREEN SALAD

DRY SAUTERNE

FRESH PINEAPPLE
FORTUNE COOKIES

1 PRELIMINARIES

Chill the wine.

Drain shrimps, and rinse under cold running water. Melt 2 tbsp. butter in a small pan. Add shrimps, and stir to mix over a *very* low flame. (Don't fry them.) Grate a little nutmeg into them, and add a few drops of lemon juice; sauté 2 minutes. Put shrimps into two small pottery or glass dishes, pour all the butter over them, and put in the refrigerator to chill.

Wash, drain, and dry the lettuce in a salad basket or on paper towels. Chill in the vegetable crisper of the refrigerator.

Peel the pineapple, removing all brown spots and thorns. Cut out the hard center core, and divide flesh lengthwise into fingers. Sprinkle with 2–3 tbsp. powdered sugar and a little Cointreau or other liqueur. Cover with plastic wrap, and chill in the refrigerator.

2 PREPARING THE MAIN DISH

INGREDIENTS:

1 frying chicken, cut in pieces	**1 small clove garlic, crushed**
Salt, pepper	**2 tbsp. soy sauce**
1 egg yolk	**4 tbsp. butter**
2 tbsp. honey	

METHOD:

Pull or cut skin off the chicken. Rinse the pieces and pat dry. Sprinkle lightly with salt and pepper. Mix together egg yolk, honey, garlic, and soy sauce in a pie tin. Roll the chicken pieces in the mixture, and place in a buttered baking dish with a lid. Dot chicken generously with butter. Cover and bake in a 350° oven until tender, 45 minutes to 1 hour.

While chicken is cooking, prepare rice according to directions on package. Stir with a fork to fluff, and stir in 1 tbsp. finely chopped parsley. Cook pea pods until just tender but still crisp. (Make sure you don't overcook them!) Drain and add 1 tbsp. butter.

3 FINAL ASSEMBLY

Tear lettuce into bite-sized pieces, and put in salad bowl. Drain mushrooms, setting aside the liquid, and arrange the mushrooms over the salad greens.

4 SERVING THE DINNER

Serve sake very warm in tiny cups or glasses. Offer potted shrimp appetizer with melba toast.

For the main course, serve Korean chicken, parsley rice, and Chinese pea pods on warmed plates.

Pour 3–4 tbsp. of the mushroom liquid over the salad; toss when brought to the table.

Pour the wine.

Dessert: pineapple fingers, with fortune cookies or plain sugar cookies.

DINNER NUMBER 25
SERVES TWO

SUPPLY CHECKLIST
Check your supply shelf for the following; if missing any item, add to marketing list:

Olive oil
Butter
Bottled gravy maker
Whole black peppercorns
Dried tarragon
French dressing
Salt, sugar

MARKETING LIST
2 slices filet mignon, 1 inch thick
1 can pâté de foie
1 lb. fresh asparagus or 1 package
    frozen asparagus spears
1 bunch green onions
1 lb. beefsteak tomatoes
1 lemon
Fresh fruit, according to season
1 package melba toast
1 loaf French bread
1 can shoestring potatoes
1 bottle brandy, preferably Cognac
    (fifth or pint)
1 bottle red Burgundy or Bordeaux

MENU

BRANDY SOUR

PÂTÉ

STEAK AU POIVRE
SHOESTRING POTATOES, ASPARAGUS
TOMATO SALAD
FRENCH BREAD

RED BURGUNDY

BOWL OF ASSORTED FRESH FRUIT

1 PRELIMINARIES

Wash and slice tomatoes. Arrange on a platter or in shallow bowl, sprinkle with 1 tsp. tarragon, and refrigerate. If using fresh asparagus, wash carefully and cut off tough white parts of stalks, leaving spears 4–5 inches long. Or peel the stalk and you won't have to cut off *any* of it.

Open can of pâté and chill.

Uncork the wine about an hour before dinner.

2 PREPARING THE MAIN DISH

INGREDIENTS:

2 slices filet mignon, 1 inch thick	1 tsp. bottled gravy maker
2 tsp. black peppercorns	4 tbsp. brandy, preferably Cognac
2 tbsp. butter	1 tbsp. water
1 tbsp. olive oil	2 tbsp. finely chopped green onion

METHOD:

Crush the peppercorns with a pestle and mortar. If you don't have a set, put the peppercorns on one half of a clean kitchen towel, fold over the other half, and crush peppercorns with a hammer, a meat tenderizer, a rolling pin, or any other weapon that seems to do the trick. With the heel of your hand, press the crushed peppercorns firmly into both sides of the steaks. Melt the butter in a heavy frying pan, and add oil. Heat until butter stops bubbling. For rare steaks, sauté 4 minutes on one side, 3 on the other; for medium, sauté 5 minutes on first side, 4 on the second. Add 1 minute each side if steaks are slightly thicker than an inch.

Remove meat to platter that has been warming in the oven. Add bottled gravy maker mixed with brandy and water to pan. Warm and stir for 1 or 2 minutes with the brown drippings in the pan. Add onion, and pour gravy over steaks.

While the steaks are cooking, simmer fresh asparagus in a small quantity of boiling salted water until just tender, approximately 8 minutes. (Don't overcook.) For frozen asparagus, follow package directions. Drain and keep warm, with 1 or 2 pats of butter placed on top.

Heat French bread wrapped in foil at 400° until crisp, about 10 minutes. Put shoestring potatoes in a shallow pan, and heat for 5–7 minutes in the oven.

Pour 2–3 tbsp. dressing on salad.

3 SERVING THE DINNER

Chill glasses. Shake the brandy sour with ice cubes, using 3 jiggers brandy, the juice of 1 lemon, and 2 tsp. sugar for two cocktails. Strain into chilled glasses. Offer pâté surrounded by melba toast.

For the main course, serve steaks, shoestring potatoes, and buttered asparagus on warmed plates along with salad.

Pour Burgundy or Bordeaux, using large wineglasses, but filling them only $\frac{1}{2}$ to $\frac{2}{3}$ full. This lets the wine's "bouquet" circulate in the glass.

Dessert: Arrange a pretty bowl of fresh fruits. Give each guest a plate to fill.

DINNER NUMBER 26
SERVES TWO

SUPPLY CHECKLIST
Check your supply shelf for the following; if missing any item, add to marketing list:
Lemon (1)
Butter
Worcestershire sauce
Sweet vermouth
Dry vermouth
Whiskey (blended, bourbon, or rye)
Angostura bitters

MARKETING LIST
1 lb. sirloin steak, ground
1 bunch parsley
1 bunch green onions
1 small green pepper
1 package frozen potato puffs
1 package frozen green beans with almonds or 1 package green beans plus small pack slivered almonds
1 package thin wheat crackers
1 small package Roquefort or Danish blue cheese
1 can smoked oysters or clams
1 lemon pie, frozen or bakery
1 bottle dry red wine, such as Paisano or Vino di Tavola
1 loaf sourdough bread

MENU

MANHATTAN

SMOKED OYSTERS

SIRLOIN SURPRISE
POTATO PUFFS, GREEN BEANS
SOURDOUGH BREAD

PAISANO

LEMON PIE

1 PRELIMINARIES

If using a frozen lemon pie, take it out of refrigerator to thaw.

Open smoked oysters or clams, drain off oil, and spear each with a toothpick. Put in a small bowl or dish, and chill in refrigerator.

Uncork the wine about an hour before dinner.

2 PREPARING THE MAIN DISH

INGREDIENTS:

1 lb. ground sirloin steak
2 1-inch cubes of Roquefort or Danish blue cheese
$\frac{3}{4}$ c. dry red wine
2 tbsp. butter
Finely chopped green onion, parsley, and green pepper, $\frac{1}{2}$ c. total
1 tbsp. Worcestershire sauce

METHOD:

Shape meat into two thick cakes around the cubes of cheese, covering the cheese completely. Heat heavy iron skillet very hot, and sear meat 2–3 minutes each side for rare, 4–5 minutes each side for medium. Remove meat to a hot buttered platter, and keep warm in oven. Turn off flame under skillet, add wine and butter, and stir well. Add chopped onion, parsley, and green pepper, and cover pan for 2 minutes, shaking to mix. Add Worcestershire sauce and stir. Pour over meat at serving time.

While meat is cooking, heat the frozen potato puffs, and cook the green beans. Wrap the sourdough bread in foil, and crisp in the oven for 10 minutes.

3 SERVING THE DINNER

Mix two Manhattan cocktails by stirring with ice cubes 3 jiggers whiskey and $\frac{1}{2}$ jigger each of sweet and dry vermouth. Add 1 dash of Angostura bitters. Strain into chilled glasses, and garnish each with a thin twist of lemon peel.

Pour the drinks. Serve the smoked oysters and a bowl of thin wheat crackers along with the cocktails.

For the main course, serve the sirloin surprise on warmed plates with green beans and potato puffs. Reheat the sauce for 1 or 2 minutes, pour over meat.

Pour the red wine into good-sized glasses.

Dessert: wedges of lemon pie.

DINNER NUMBER 27
SERVES FOUR

Check your supply shelf for the following; if missing any item, add to marketing list:

Olive oil
Butter
Sweet vermouth
Espresso, instant or ground
Eggs (3)
Whole black peppercorns

MARKETING LIST
½ lb. bacon
Salad greens: lettuce, escarole, curly
        chicory, and green onions
        (optional)
2 lemons
1 bunch parsley
1 jar grated Romano cheese
1 jar grated Parmesan cheese
1 1-lb. package spaghetti
1 package breadsticks
1 bottle Italian dressing
1 can or jar marinated artichoke
        hearts or 1 package frozen
        artichoke hearts
1 pint raspberry sherbet
2 bottles dry Italian white wine,
        such as Soave or white Chianti
1 bottle Strega (Italian liqueur)
1 quart club soda

MENU

SWEET VERMOUTH AND SODA

MARINATED ARTICHOKE HEARTS
BREADSTICKS

SPAGHETTI CARBONARA
MIXED GREEN SALAD

SOAVE

RASPBERRY SHERBET
ESPRESSO AND STREGA

1 PRELIMINARIES

Chill the white wine.

If using frozen artichoke hearts, cook according to directions, drain, and chill. When they are cool, grind a little black pepper over them, and sprinkle with a dressing of 3 tbsp. oil mixed with 1 tbsp. lemon juice. Refrigerate until serving time. Wash and drain salad greens, discarding tough or bruised outside leaves. Wrap in paper towels, and put in the vegetable crisper of refrigerator.

2 PREPARING THE MAIN DISH

INGREDIENTS:

1 lb. spaghetti
3 eggs, beaten
⅓ c. grated Romano cheese
⅓ c. grated Parmesan cheese

6 slices bacon, diced
3 tbsp. olive oil
⅓ c. dry white wine
Salt, freshly ground black pepper

METHOD:

Have a *large* pot ¾ full of boiling salted water (use 2 tbsp. salt—it has to season the spaghetti). Add 1 tbsp. oil. Put in the spaghetti, and cook 7–8 minutes *after* the water returns to a boil. The spaghetti should still be slightly firm when you bite it—that is, *al dente*.

While spaghetti is cooking, beat 3 eggs with grated Romano and Parmesan cheese. Heat 2 tbsp. olive oil in a skillet, and fry diced bacon until crisp. Add the wine, and continue cooking until wine evaporates. Drain spaghetti.

The remaining procedures should be done at the last minute, *after* you serve drinks and appetizers, as spaghetti gets sticky if it stands. Return spaghetti to the saucepan, which must be *hot;* add the egg-cheese mixture, the hot bacon-oil mixture, and plenty of pepper. Stir rapidly so egg mixture cooks onto hot spaghetti.

3 SERVING THE DINNER

Put ice cubes into four goblet-shaped glasses. Pour 2 jiggers sweet vermouth into each, add a twist of lemon peel, and fill with club soda.

Serve artichoke hearts on individual plates garnished with 1 or 2 sprigs of parsley. Arrange breadsticks on a tray, and serve with a plate of sweet butter.

For the main course, serve spaghetti carbonara very hot on warmed plates, along with green salad with 3 tbsp. Italian dressing mixed in.

Dessert: raspberry sherbet followed by espresso in demitasse cups and Strega.

DINNER NUMBER 28
SERVES FOUR

SUPPLY CHECKLIST
Check your supply shelf for the following; if missing any item, add to marketing list:
Butter
Flour
Sugar
Paprika
Curry powder
Cinnamon
Salt, pepper
Bottled French or Italian dressing
Vodka
Dry vermouth

MARKETING LIST
1 large frying chicken, cut in pieces, approximately 3 lbs.
$\frac{1}{4}$ lb. smoked salmon
2 avocados
1 medium-size red onion
1 medium-size white onion
2 lemons
4–6 large pears or 1 large can pear halves
1 package cracked wheat pilaf
1 package pumpernickel slices
1 package croissants
1 can chicken broth
2 bottles Grenache rosé or sparkling rosé wine
$\frac{1}{2}$ bottle red table-wine for cooking pears

MENU

VODKA MARTINI

SMOKED SALMON

CHICKEN MARILI
CRACKED WHEAT PILAF, AVOCADO SALAD
CROISSANTS

GRENACHE ROSÉ

PEARS

1 PRELIMINARIES

Chill the rosé wine in the refrigerator.

If using fresh pears, cut them in half, peel, and scoop out core and stringy center sections. Dip them in a mixture of $\frac{1}{2}$ c. water and 1 tbsp. lemon juice to prevent discoloration. In an enameled skillet or shallow casserole, combine $\frac{1}{2}$ c. sugar and $1\frac{1}{2}$ c. red wine. Heat, and simmer for 5 minutes. Put pears into the wine, cover, and cook gently until tender but not mushy. Take out the pears, put them in a serving bowl, and continue cooking the juice until it reduces and becomes more syrupy. Pour the juice over the pears and chill. If using canned pears, add no sugar. Mix 1 c. of the juice from the can with 1 c. red wine. Warm the pears in this juice for 10–15 minutes on a very low flame, so that the liquid is below boiling point. (Canned pears don't need cooking; they're already tender.) Take out the pears, and reduce the juice by boiling for a few minutes. Then pour juice over the fruit in a serving bowl. If using a glass bowl, cool the syrup a little to avoid any risk of cracking the glass.) Refrigerate.

Peel avocados, remove seeds, and cut in sections. Arrange on a salad platter or shallow bowl, and scatter paper-thin rings of red and white onion over them. Sprinkle with a sharp bottled dressing, and refrigerate.

Cut pumpernickel into small squares, butter thinly, and arrange pieces of smoked salmon on each. Cover with plastic wrap to prevent drying.

2 PREPARING THE MAIN DISH

INGREDIENTS:

$\frac{1}{2}$ c. flour	Cinnamon
Salt, pepper	1 large frying chicken, cut in pieces
1 tsp. paprika	$\frac{1}{2}$ stick butter
$\frac{1}{2}$ tsp. curry powder	1 c. chicken broth

METHOD:

Mix flour, salt, pepper, paprika, curry powder, and dash of cinnamon in a brown paper bag. Shake chicken pieces in the bag to coat them with the mixture.

Melt butter in a skillet (one with a cover), and sauté chicken pieces briefly until golden. Remove chicken pieces, and set aside on a warm plate. Add 1 tbsp. of flour remaining in bag to juices in skillet, stir quickly, then pour in chicken broth and stir over low heat until blended. Return chicken pieces to skillet, put lid on, and bake in a 350° oven for 45 minutes, or until tender. (When you prick it with a fork, juices run yellow.)

While chicken is cooking, prepare cracked wheat pilaf as package says.

Warm the croissants in the oven.

3 SERVING THE DINNER

Chill the cocktail glasses. Stir the martinis in a pitcher with ice cubes, using 6 jiggers vodka to 1½ of dry vermouth. Strain into chilled cocktail glasses, or serve on the rocks with a twist of lemon. If you want seconds, mix a fresh batch when you need it rather than double the quantities. Martinis that stand around get watery, so don't risk serving an inferior second drink—start over. Serve the smoked salmon on pumpernickel with the cocktails.

For the main course, serve the chicken Marili with the cracked wheat pilaf on warmed plates. Bring out the avocado-onion salad, and pass around a basket of hot rolls.

Pour the chilled rosé wine.

Dessert: pears in wine syrup.

DINNER NUMBER 29
SERVES TWO

SUPPLY CHECKLIST
Check your supply shelf for the following; if missing any item, add to marketing list:

Lemon
Butter (1 stick plus 2 tbsp.)
Bottled steak sauce (A.1. or other)
Garlic
Dried basil or tarragon
Salad dressing
Sugar (superfine granulated)
Salt, pepper
Crème de menthe or other liqueur
Whiskey (blended, Scotch, or
 bourbon)

MARKETING LIST
10–12 uncooked jumbo shrimps, about
 $1\frac{1}{4}$ lbs.
$\frac{1}{4}$ lb. thinly sliced prosciutto
1 lb. tomatoes
1 cantaloupe or honeydew melon
1 bunch green onions
1 package rice (white, long grain)
1 loaf French bread
1 pint lemon sherbet
1 bottle light, dry Italian white wine

MENU

WHISKEY SOUR

MELON

SCAMPI GUADALAJARA
BUTTERED RICE, SLICED TOMATO SALAD
FRENCH BREAD

ITALIAN WHITE WINE

LEMON SHERBET

1 PRELIMINARIES

Chill the white wine.

Wash and slice the tomatoes, arrange on a salad platter, and sprinkle with basil (tarragon may be substituted for basil). Chill in refrigerator.

Cut sections of melon. Peel, and arrange slices of prosciutto ham over them. Cover with plastic wrap and chill.

2 PREPARING THE MAIN DISH

INGREDIENTS:

10–12 jumbo shrimps, raw	1½ tbsp. A.1. or other steak sauce
2 green onions	1 tbsp. lemon juice
1 stick butter	¼ tsp. each salt and coarsely ground
2 crushed garlic cloves	black pepper

METHOD:

Carefully shell the shrimps, leaving on the last sections of shells and the tails. (If you take off *all* the shell, the tails will fall off.) Remove the veins down the backs. With a sharp knife, slit the shrimps almost but not quite through, and spread open. It's a good idea to weight them down for a while under a flat plate or tin with something heavy on top, so they will lie flat.

Chop finely the white part of the onions. Soften butter at room temperature. Beat together the butter, onions, garlic, steak sauce, lemon juice, salt, and pepper. Melt over low heat, stirring to mix ingredients. Keep warm, but do not allow to brown.

Cook the rice next, as it takes longer than the shrimps. When ready, fluff with a fork and add 2 tbsp. butter. Cover the pan with a clean dish towel or paper towel, put the lid back on, and set in a warm place till serving time.

Turn on the broiler. Arrange shrimps, split sides up, in a greased baking dish, and broil 4 inches from a high flame for 5 minutes. At serving time, pour the hot butter sauce over them.

Wrap the French bread in foil, and warm in a 400° oven for 10 minutes.

3 SERVING THE DINNER

Chill tulip-shaped glasses. For 2 whiskey sours, shake well with ice 3 jiggers whiskey, the juice of 1 lemon, 2 tsp. sugar (sugar may be increased or decreased to taste). Strain into chilled glasses.

Serve melon with prosciutto.

For the main course, serve the scampi Guadalajara with the butter sauce poured over them, accompanied by rice on warmed plates.

Sprinkle tomato salad with 3–4 tbsp. bottled dressing. Cut French bread into slices and put in a basket.

Pour white wine.

Dessert: lemon sherbet topped with crème de menthe.

DINNER NUMBER 30
SERVES TWO

MENU

SILVER FIZZ

JELLIED CONSOMMÉ

KIDNEYS VERT PRÉ
RAMEKINS OF MASHED POTATO
MIXED GREEN SALAD
HARD ROLLS

BEAUJOLAIS

NAPOLEONS

SUPPLY CHECKLIST
Check your supply shelf for the following; if missing any item, add to marketing list:

Butter
Olive oil
Egg (1)
Dried thyme
Dried tarragon
Dry mustard
Mace or nutmeg
Red wine vinegar
Salt, pepper, paprika
Grated Parmesan cheese
Gin
Powdered sugar

MARKETING LIST
6 lamb kidneys or 2 veal kidneys (buy them *whole* if possible, or you may find they have been split unevenly)
Salad greens, 2 or 3 different kinds, such as escarole, watercress, lettuce, endive
2 lemons
1 lime
1 bunch parsley
1 bunch green onions
1 bunch chives
1 bunch fresh chervil, if available
1 small package instant mashed potatoes
1 can beef consommé
1 bottle dressing, California-French style
2 Napoleons or other pâtisseries
1 bottle Beaujolais or Napa Valley Burgundy

1 PRELIMINARIES

The night before, put the consommé in the coldest part of the refrigerator so it will jell.

The night of the dinner, wash, drain, and dry the salad greens and put in refrigerator. (You will only need to use part of each head or bunch. Put the rest in the vegetable crisper for another meal.)

Prepare instant mashed potatoes according to package directions, adding the yolk of 1 egg (retain the white) to the milk you use in mixing—potatoes will brown better. Put the seasoned mashed potatoes in small buttered ramekins or tiny casseroles, drizzle on a little melted butter, then sprinkle with grated Parmesan cheese and a little paprika. Set aside while preparing the main dish.

Uncork the wine about an hour before dinner.

2 PREPARING THE MAIN DISH

INGREDIENTS:

6 lamb kidneys or 2 veal kidneys
4 tbsp. butter at room temperature
½ tsp. each minced parsley, chervil,
    tarragon, chives
1 green onion, minced, white part only

¼ c. (4 tbsp.) olive oil
Salt, pepper
Pinch each of thyme, dry mustard, mace
    (or nutmeg)

METHOD:

Preheat oven to broil.

Mix butter with minced herbs and green onion. The easiest way to do this is to mash with a fork on a chopping board. When well blended, form it in a long narrow roll, wrap in waxed paper and store in refrigerator. That way it's easy to divide equally when garnishing the kidneys.

Cut the kidneys in half carefully, starting from the rounded side. With a small pair of scissors (curved nail scissors are fine for this job), cut out all the white core and tubes, and pull off the thin, tissue-like outer skin. Toss kidneys in a bowl with olive oil and seasonings until they are well coated with the mixture.

Put potato ramekins in the upper part of the oven to brown. Place kidneys cut sides down on broiler rack, and broil 4 inches from flame for 5 minutes. Turn and broil 3 more minutes.

While kidneys are broiling, tear salad greens into bite-size pieces. Put into a wooden or pottery bowl, and chill.

3 FINAL ASSEMBLY

Make the silver fizz in a blender if you have one, otherwise in a shaker. For two drinks, use 3 jiggers gin, juice of 1 lemon and ½ lime, 1 egg white, and 1½ tbsp. powdered sugar. If using a blender, add crushed ice, about ⅔ c. drained. Blend until white and frothy. If using a shaker, add ice cubes, and shake very vigorously.

Remove kidneys from broiler when done. Check to see if potato ramekins are brown. If not, turn oven to low and let them cook longer. If they *are* brown, turn the oven off; there will be enough heat left to keep them piping hot. The kidneys should be kept warm on a platter or pie plate over a pan of hot water; cover.

4 SERVING THE DINNER

Serve the silver fizz in large, stemmed cocktail glasses or in wineglasses.

Spoon jellied consommé into soup cups with wedges of lemon.

For the main course, serve kidneys Vert Pré with a dab of herbed butter in the middle of each one, on warmed plates, accompanied by the potato ramekins.

Pour 3–4 tbsp. dressing over the green salad. Toss before serving.

Pour the Beaujolais or American Burgundy.

Dessert: Napoleons.

DINNER NUMBER 31
SERVES TWO

SUPPLY CHECKLIST
Check your supply shelf for the following; if missing any item, add to marketing list:

Oil
Sherry ($\frac{1}{4}$ c.)
Salt, pepper
Garlic
Dried oregano
Lemons (2)
Onion (1)

MARKETING LIST
10 squares lean boneless lamb, 1$\frac{1}{2}$ inch square
1 head lettuce or escarole
1 bunch carrots
1 green pepper
1 lb. or 1 basket cherry tomatoes
1 package frozen eggplant
1 package dried figs
1 box whole dates
1 can stuffed vine leaves
1 package rice pilaf mix
1 loaf Middle Eastern pita bread (or French bread)
1 small box rahat lokoum ("Turkish Delight")
1 or 2 small packages halvah
1 lb. walnuts, almonds, or hazelnuts in shell
1 can ($\frac{1}{2}$ lb.) Turkish-style coffee
1 bottle raki (or substitute Greek ouzo, if you wish)
1 bottle Pinot Noir or other red wine

MENU

TURKISH RAKI

STUFFED VINE LEAVES

LAMB SHISH KEBAB
RICE PILAF, EGGPLANT STICKS
GREEN SALAD
PITA BREAD

RED WINE

ASSORTMENT OF NUTS, DRIED FRUIT
AND TURKISH-STYLE CANDIES
TURKISH COFFEE

1 PRELIMINARIES

The night before the party, marinate the meat according to directions below ("Preparing the Main Dish").

About two hours before the dinner wash, drain, and dry the lettuce or escarole. Tear into bite-size pieces, and arrange in a salad bowl. Wash and scrape 2 carrots, and grate them into long thin shreds over the lettuce. Refrigerate.

Make a dressing with 3 tbsp. oil, 1 tbsp. lemon juice, $\frac{1}{2}$ tsp. salt, and a little black pepper. Shake in a screw-top jar.

Uncork the wine about an hour before dinner.

2 PREPARING THE MAIN DISH

INGREDIENTS:

10 squares lamb, 1$\frac{1}{2}$ inches on each side (if the butcher can't or won't prepare them for you, buy a small leg of lamb and cut the squares yourself; any extra pieces can be used for another meal)
1 onion, minced

$\frac{1}{2}$ tsp. salt
1 clove garlic, crushed
$\frac{1}{4}$ c. sherry
$\frac{1}{4}$ c. oil
1 tbsp. dried oregano
1 green pepper, cut in 1-inch squares
6–8 cherry tomatoes

METHOD:

Crush onion with salt in a bowl. Stir in garlic, sherry, oil, and oregano. Add lamb squares to this marinade, stirring well to coat them all over, and let marinate in the refrigerator for at least twenty-four hours. Many of the best Turkish chefs do not marinate the meat for shish kebab at all, but they use very tender young lamb, which makes marinating less necessary.

Drain meat from marinade and thread on long skewers, alternating meat squares with pieces of green pepper. (Put cherry tomatoes on separate skewer.) Do not push too close together—the meat should not touch the peppers. Cook on a barbecue or hibachi over hot coals for approximately 6–8 minutes on each side. Put tomato skewer on after meat is half cooked. To cook in the stove, broil 4 inches from high flame for 8 minutes on the first side, then turn and broil another 6 minutes.

As soon as you have put the meat on, prepare the rice pilaf, and cook the frozen eggplant according to directions on each package.

3 FINAL ASSEMBLY

Arrange dessert platter, using dates, figs, nuts, and squares of halvah and rahat lokoum in a pretty pattern.

Heat and crisp French or Syrian bread wrapped in foil at 350° in the oven for 5 or 10 minutes.

4 SERVING THE DINNER

Pour raki or ouzo over ice cubes in old-fashioned glasses; bring a small pitcher of iced water to dilute it if desired. Water gives the clear liquid a milky look. Raki and ouzo have a characteristic anise flavor; if you don't enjoy it, offer sherry on the rocks instead. With the drinks offer the stuffed vine leaves on small plates with sections of lemon to squeeze over them . . . with salad forks, or toothpicks.

Serve the shish kebab on top of rice pilaf on hot plates, with eggplant alongside. Pour dressing over salad, and toss. Offer chunks of hot French or Syrian bread, and pour the red wine.

Dessert: Present the dessert platter. As halvah and dates are sticky, and rahat lokoum is covered with powdered sugar, it would be a nice touch to offer finger bowls of water, with a few flower petals scattered on them or floating a thin lemon slice, so that sticky fingers may be rinsed. Any small glass bowl such as Chinese rice bowls will serve the purpose and add a touch of glamour.

To make Turkish coffee, you need the proper small, tapered brass coffee pot, which can be bought in most Middle Eastern specialty shops; if you don't have one, substitute instant espresso coffee.

DINNER NUMBER 32
SERVES TWO

SUPPLY CHECKLIST
Check your supply shelf for the following; if missing any item, add to marketing list:

Butter
Flour
Chicken bouillon cubes
Salt, pepper, paprika
Mayonnaise
Kahlúa liqueur (or crème de cacao)
Vodka
Lemon

MARKETING LIST
4–6 chicken legs or 1 package frozen
       chicken legs
1 lettuce, small
1 avocado
1 lb. onions
1 small cream cheese
1 8-oz. carton sour cream
1 can smoked oysters
1 package medium noodles
1 package bake-and-serve biscuits
1 can grapefruit sections
1 small jar poppy seeds
1 small can black olives
1 package melba toast rounds
1 pint coffee ice cream
1 bottle Almadén Mountain White
       Chablis or other dry white
       wine

MENU

VODKA

SMOKED OYSTERS SUPREME

LEGS FAIR AND FOWL
BUTTERED NOODLES
AVOCADO-GRAPEFRUIT SALAD
HOT BISCUITS

CHABLIS

COFFEE ICE CREAM

1 PRELIMINARIES

Chill wine in refrigerator.

Wash, drain, and dry enough lettuce leaves to line two salad plates. Drain grapefruit sections, saving 3 tbsp. of the juice. Peel and section avocado. Arrange grapefruit and avocado sections alternately on lettuce-lined plates. Thin ¼ c. mayonnaise with the reserved grapefruit juice, and pour over salad. Refrigerate.

Prepare appetizer. Drain smoked oysters, and chop them. Pit and chop coarsly 8 black olives. Mash cream cheese with a fork. Mix together olives, cream cheese, and smoked oysters, and pack into a small dish or bowl. On top, put a layer of paper-thin rings of onion. Cover with plastic wrap and chill in the refrigerator until serving time.

2 PREPARING THE MAIN DISH

INGREDIENTS:

4–6 chicken legs or 1 defrosted package frozen legs
¾ c. chopped onion
½ stick butter
2 tbsp. flour
½ tsp. salt
1 c. chicken broth (from 1 bouillon cube)
1 tsp. paprika
1 c. sour cream

METHOD:

Sauté the chopped onion slowly in the butter until golden, stirring often. Lay the chicken legs over the onion, cover, turn heat low, and cook 25 minutes, turning once after 15 minutes. Sprinkle flour and salt over contents of pan. Add chicken broth, and continue cooking until tender, about 25 minutes more. Remove from fire. Stir in paprika and sour cream over and around the legs, and heat gently over a very low flame.

While chicken is cooking, put noodles in boiling salted water, and cook until just tender according to time directions on package. Drain and add 2 tbsp. butter and 1 tbsp. poppy seeds. Toss and mix before serving. Bake biscuits in a hot oven according to package directions.

3 SERVING THE DINNER

Pour 2 oz. vodka (that's about $1\frac{1}{3}$ jiggers full) over ice in each guest's old-fashioned glass. Add a twist of lemon and a little water if desired. Serve bowl of smoked oysters supreme as appetizer, accompanied by melba toast rounds.

For the main course, serve chicken legs in sour cream sauce on warmed plates, along with the buttered poppy-seed noodles. Offer avocado-grapefruit salad. Arrange hot biscuits and butter pats or curls on a tray, or split biscuits and butter them in the kitchen. Pour the wine.

Dessert: Put a scoop of coffee ice cream in each dessert dish. With the handle of a wooden spoon, poke a hole in the top of each scoop, and fill with Kahlúa or crème de cacao just before serving.

DINNER NUMBER 33
Valentine Dinner
SERVES TWO

SUPPLY CHECKLIST
Check your supply shelf for the following; if missing any item, add to marketing list:

Egg (1)
Grated Parmesan cheese
Milk
Butter
Oil
Red wine vinegar
Lemon (1)
Salt, pepper, paprika
Dried or fresh basil

MARKETING LIST
2 large lobster tails (frozen)
2 small filets mignons
1 lb. ripe tomatoes
2 large, ripe peaches
1 package small hard bake-and-serve rolls
1 can consommé madrilene
1 8-oz. carton sour cream
1 jar béarnaise sauce (if you can't find béarnaise, buy 1 jar hollandaise sauce and see instructions below)
1 jar red caviar, imported or American, smallest size
1 bottle Spanish sherry, Amontillado or Tio Pepe
1 bottle dry champagne, Almadén Blanc de Blancs or Great Western Brut

MENU

SHERRY

JELLIED MADRILENE WITH CAVIAR

LOVABLE LOBSTER
POTATOES CHANTILLY, TOMATO SALAD
SMALL HARD ROLLS

CHAMPAGNE

PEACHES IN CHAMPAGNE

1 PRELIMINARIES

Chill champagne overnight. It must be *really* cold.

Chill canned madrilene so it is firmly jelled.

Peel tomatoes by dipping for a few seconds into boiling water, after which skins will pull off easily. Slice and arrange on a serving plate. Sprinkle with oil, red wine vinegar, freshly ground black pepper, and fresh or dried basil. Refrigerate.

Prepare three servings of instant mashed potatoes according to package directions. Beat in one whole raw egg and 4 tbsp. grated Parmesan cheese. Spoon into a flat baking dish. Sprinkle paprika on top in the shape of a heart. Set aside while preparing main course; brown in oven later.

2 PREPARING THE MAIN DISH

INGREDIENTS:

2 small filets mignons, 1–1½ inches thick
2 large lobster tails, thawed

Béarnaise sauce, bottled

METHOD:

If béarnaise sauce is not available, use hollandaise sauce and season as follows: In a very small pan or skillet, put 3 tbsp. of red wine vinegar and 1 tbsp. water. Add 1 tbsp. of dried tarragon and 2 tbsp. of very finely chopped green onion. Simmer until reduced and almost syrupy. Cool a little, and stir into hollandaise sauce. Add a sprinkling of pepper, and heat according to directions on jar. Sauce must not be overheated or it will separate.

Wrap a lobster tail around the outside of each filet, fastening with small skewers to hold in place. They may be broiled over charcoal, in a rotisserie, or in the broiler of the stove. If you are using the stove for the main dish, brown the potatoes first, 5 minutes under the broiler, and heat the rolls in the oven according to package directions. Then put the potatoes in the oven to keep hot, and proceed to broil the lobster-filets. These will take 7–8 minutes, 3 inches away from flame, according to the degree of rareness desired, or 5–8 minutes over charcoal. Turn once during cooking.

While lobster-wrapped filets are cooking, peel and pit the peaches and put into two goblets. Pierce each one several times with a fork, and refrigerate.

3 SERVING THE DINNER

Pour sherry into small-stemmed glasses. It will have more flavor if not served ice-cold, but this is a matter of individual preference.

Stir the jellied madrilene, add a squeeze of lemon juice, stir again, and spoon into two soup cups or small bowls. Top each serving with a dollop of sour cream, and on top of the cream put a tiny spoonful of red caviar. Put the hard rolls on the table.

For the main course, serve the Lovable Lobster, accompanied by the potatoes Chantilly and tomato salad. Béarnaise sauce may be spooned over the filets before serving or offered separately.

Pour champagne over the chilled peaches, and bring the bottle to the table to serve throughout the meal, replenishing the wine as needed.

Dessert: peaches, soaked in what is left of the champagne.

DINNER NUMBER 34
SERVES TWO

SUPPLY CHECKLIST
Check your supply shelf for the following; if missing any items, add to marketing list:

Butter
Garlic
Salt, pepper
Lemons (2)
Scotch whiskey
Vermouth, dry

MARKETING LIST
2 lamb steaks, about 1 lb. without
    bone
1 head lettuce, escarole or romaine
1 green pepper
1 package frozen spinach soufflé
1 bunch parsley
2 large ripe bananas
1 jar marinated artichoke hearts
1 8-oz. can tomato sauce
1 package rice (white, long grain,
    not instant)
1 package shredded coconut
1 8-oz. carton sour cream
2 portions smoked trout, chub, or
    whitefish from delicatessen
    counter, or 1 can smoked
    trout fillets
1 loaf French bread

MENU

ROB ROY

SMOKED TROUT, CHUB, OR WHITEFISH

LAMBALAYA
SPINACH SOUFFLÉ, GREEN SALAD
GARLIC BREAD

CALIFORNIA CABERNET

CRUNCHY BANANAS

1 PRELIMINARIES

Wash, drain, and dry salad greens. Use a few of the leaves to line two small plates. Arrange smoked fish (trout, chub, or whitefish) on the lettuce-lined plates, and chill in refrigerator.

Tear the rest of the lettuce into bite-size pieces. Drain the artichoke hearts from the marinade, saving the liquid. Cut artichoke hearts in half, and arrange over salad greens. Chill in refrigerator.

Uncork the wine about an hour before dinner.

2 PREPARING THE MAIN DISH

INGREDIENTS:

2 lamb steaks	**2 tbsp. butter**
$\frac{1}{2}$ c. regular rice	**$\frac{1}{2}$ of 8-oz. can tomato sauce**
1$\frac{1}{2}$ c. boiling water	**1 green pepper, cut in 1 inch squares**
$\frac{1}{2}$ tsp. salt	**1 clove garlic, crushed (optional)**
$\frac{1}{4}$ tsp. pepper	

METHOD:

Trim bone, fat, and skin from lamb, and cut the meat in squares. Stir the dry rice into the boiling water with the salt, pepper, and butter. Add all the rest of the ingredients, cover, and cook very gently over low heat for $\frac{1}{2}$ hour, until the lamb is tender and the rice cooked. If necessary, add a little more tomato sauce to prevent sticking.

While the lamb is cooking, heat the spinach soufflé in the oven, and prepare garlic bread as follows: Slash the French bread diagonally at 1-inch intervals almost through to the bottom. Spread softened butter between the slices, and put a thin sliver of garlic in each cut. Wrap in foil, and heat for 10 to 20 minutes in 350° oven.

Spread the coconut in a shallow layer in a baking tin, and toast in the oven until golden: (It only takes a few minutes; don't let it scorch.)

3 FINAL ASSEMBLY

Add a little lemon juice to the marinade from the artichokes, pour over salad, and toss to mix.

Peel bananas, and cut in 1-inch pieces. Dip the pieces in sour cream, and roll in toasted coconut. Arrange on two dessert plates, and refrigerate until serving.

Chop 1 tbsp. parsley to garnish lambalaya.

Mix two dry Rob Roys by shaking with ice 3 jiggers Scotch with 1 jigger dry vermouth. Strain over ice cubes in old-fashioned glass, add a twist of lemon peel to each drink.

4 SERVING THE DINNER

Serve Rob Roys.

Offer smoked trout, chub, or white-fish with quarter of lemon to squeeze over it.

For the main course, bring out the lambalaya sprinkled with a little chopped parsley on a warmed plate, accompanied by the spinach soufflé. Serve green salad with artichokes. Unwrap the garlic bread, and separate slices into a basket.

Pour the wine.

Dessert: crunchy bananas.

DINNER NUMBER 35
SERVES SIX TO EIGHT

Check your supply shelf for the following; if missing any item, add to marketing list:

Butter
Flour
Salt
Nutmeg
Egg (1)
Parmesan cheese
Honey
Italian dressing

MARKETING LIST
$1-1\frac{1}{4}$ lb. cooked turkey roll from
      delicatessen (or use leftovers
      from roast turkey)
1 package heat-and-serve butter-
      flake rolls
2 bunches watercress
1 lb. Belgian endive
1 green pepper
$\frac{1}{2}$ lb. fresh mushrooms
3 or 4 large grapefruits
1 8-oz. package spaghetti
2 cans chicken or turkey broth
1 package slivered almonds
$\frac{1}{2}$ pint light cream
1 package frozen raspberries
1 quart peach sherbet or Dutch
      apple ice cream
1 bottle Marsala or medium-dry
      sherry
3 bottles champagne or sparkling
      Vouvray

MENU

MARSALA OR SHERRY

HONEY-BROILED GRAPEFRUIT

TURKEY TETRAZZINI
ENDIVE AND WATERCRESS SALAD
HOT BUTTERFLAKE ROLLS

CHAMPAGNE

PEACH SHERBET

1 PRELIMINARIES

Cut grapefruit in half, and loosen each section from the membrane with a serrated grapefruit knife. Warm 4 tbsp. honey with 1 tbsp. Marsala or sherry, and stir to mix. Brush top of each grapefruit with the mixture just before broiling.

Wash watercress, and remove any coarse stems. Wrap in a towel, and chill in the refrigerator. Remove outer leaves of endive, wash, and dry. Cut in ¾-inch slices and chill.

Chill champagne or Vouvray, overnight if possible. It should be served very cold, and a wine cooler helps keep it that way. But if you don't have one, a less glamorous ice bucket will do as well.

Partly defrost the raspberries, and put them in the blender for a few seconds. Keep them very cold, either in the refrigerator or in the freezing compartment.

2 PREPARING THE MAIN DISH

INGREDIENTS:

- **8 oz. spaghetti**
- **1 tsp. salt**
- **¼ tsp. nutmeg**
- **¼ c. butter (½ stick)**
- **2 c. canned chicken or turkey broth**
- **1 c. light cream**
- **¼ c. Marsala or sherry**
- **¼ c. shredded Parmesan cheese**
- **2 c. cooked turkey, cut in 1-inch cubes**
- **¼ c. chopped green pepper**
- **½ lb. sliced mushrooms**
- **1 egg yolk**
- **½ c. slivered almonds**
- **1 bottle Italian dressing**

METHOD:

Preheat oven to 350°. Break spaghetti into 2-inch pieces, and drop into 6 c. rapidly boiling salted water. Bring to boil again. Stir constantly with wooden spoon or fork. Cover, and remove from heat. Allow to stand for 10 minutes. Then drain in colander, and transfer to a warm buttered bowl.

Melt butter in a saucepan over low heat. Blend in flour, salt, and nutmeg, and stir with a wooden spoon until smooth and bubbly. Remove from heat. Stir in broth and cream, then bring to a boil, stirring, for one minute. (A whisk is the best implement for beating and stirring, as it prevents the sauce from getting lumpy.) Next stir in the wine and cheese, and when well blended, add the sauce to the spaghetti.

Add cubed turkey and green pepper. Wash and slice the mushrooms, and add them, along with the lightly beaten egg yolk. Blend all together thoroughly. Pour mixture into a buttered bake-and-serve dish, and sprinkle with almonds. Bake un-covered at 350° for 25–30 minutes. Remove and allow to stand for 10 minutes.

While turkey tetrazzini is baking, heat the butterflake rolls. Wrap them in foil to warm while you serve drinks.

3 FINAL ASSEMBLY

Separate watercress into smaller sprigs, and mix with sliced endive in a large salad bowl. Sprinkle over it about $\frac{1}{3}$ c. Italian dressing. Refrigerate until serving time. Brush grapefruit halves with the honey-wine mixture, and put under broiler until they caramelize a little on top, about 5–10 minutes. Turn oven to lowest possible heat, or leave the oven door open, to keep things hot until ready to serve.

4 SERVING THE DINNER

Serve Marsala or sherry in small tulip-shaped wineglasses.

Bring out the broiled grapefruit.

For the main course, bring out the turkey tetrazzini in the baking dish, and make certain dinner plates are really warm.

Toss and mix the salad.

Put hot butterflake rolls in a basket. Pour the champagne, leaving the second bottle in the refrigerator or wine cooler until you are ready to pour.

Dessert: peach sherbet or Dutch apple ice cream with a topping of puréed raspberries.

DINNER NUMBER 36
SERVES FOUR

MENU

SIDECAR

COLD STUFFED TOMATOES

FILET MIGNON CHARLEVILLE
SHOESTRING POTATOES, GREEN BEANS
TOSSED GREEN SALAD
SOURDOUGH FRENCH ROLLS

FRENCH BURGUNDY

SLICED PEACHES

1 PRELIMINARIES

Wash, drain, and dry the salad greens. Wrap them in a towel, and chill in the refrigerator.

Cut a ½-inch lid off the top of each tomato, and using a small teaspoon, scoop out all the juice and seeds. Turn tomatoes upside down to drain. Take the herring fillets out of the cream, and cut into smaller pieces about ¾ inch square. Chill the tomatoes, the herring fillets, and the remains of the cream. Thaw frozen peaches, or if you are using fresh ones, peel, slice, and sprinkle them with 4 tbsp. sugar and 2 tbsp. lemon juice. Chill.

Uncork the wine at least an hour before dinner.

2 PREPARING THE MAIN DISH

INGREDIENTS:
4 1-inch-thick slices filet mignon
½ lb. fresh mushrooms
3 tbsp. lightly salted (regular) butter
1 tbsp. each brandy, Madeira, and sherry
1 tsp. flour
¼ c. sweet butter
1 tbsp. Dijon-style mustard
Salt

METHOD:
Wash mushrooms gently, and cut off any hard stem bottoms. If the skin is white and unblemished, it is not necessary to peel. Slice the mushrooms, and sauté in the 3 tbsp. butter for 5 minutes. Mix brandy, Madeira, and sherry, pour into pan, stir, and ignite. Allow flames to die down. Sprinkle flour over mushrooms, stir in sweet butter until melted, and then stir in mustard. Continue stirring until sauce thickens slightly; keep warm over very low flame. Heat a cast-iron skillet very hot, and sprinkle lightly with salt. Pan broil filet slices 4 minutes on one side, 3 minutes on the other, for medium rare. As soon as you have put the meat in the pan, cook the green beans according to package directions, and heat the French rolls and the shoestring potatoes. When the filet is ready, take it out of the skillet or it will go on cooking, and keep warm either on a plate over hot, but not boiling, water, or on a rack in the oven over the lowest possible heat.

3 FINAL ASSEMBLY

Tear up salad greens, and put in a large wooden or pottery bowl. Fill tomatoes with herring pieces; pour some of the remaining cream on the top of each. Put on small plates, and garnish with a sprig of chicory or parsley. Make 2 sidecar cocktails by mixing together 4 jiggers brandy, 2 jiggers Cointreau, and 2 jiggers lemon juice. Shake well with ice, and strain into cocktail glasses.

4 SERVING THE DINNER

Follow cocktails with stuffed tomato appetizer.

Serve the filets mignons on warmed plates, with shoestring potatoes and green beans, and spoon the hot mushroom-mustard sauce over each filet. Pour well-shaken Roquefort dressing over the salad; toss and mix at the table. Serve hot French rolls. Pour the wine.

Dessert: peach slices in small bowls with 1 tsp. of Cointreau sprinkled over each serving.

DINNER NUMBER 37
SERVES TWO

MENU

SWEET VERMOUTH AND SODA

ANTIPASTO

VEAL SCALOPPINE MARSALA
SPINACH NOODLES
GREEN SALAD
ITALIAN BREAD

ITALIAN WHITE WINE

SPUMONI
ESPRESSO

SUPPLY CHECKLIST
Check your supply shelf for the following; if missing any item, add to marketing list:

Butter
Olive oil
Flour
Egg (1)
Dry bread crumbs
Salt, pepper
Garlic

MARKETING LIST
4 very thin veal cutlets (ask the butcher to cut them from the leg, for scaloppine; they should weigh $\frac{1}{2}$ to $\frac{3}{4}$ lbs. all together, no more)
$\frac{1}{4}$ lb. thinly sliced Italian salami
$\frac{1}{4}$ lb. prosciutto, thinly sliced
1 bunch green onions
1 bunch fresh chives
1 head lettuce
1 small basket cherry tomatoes
1 head escarole or romaine
1 loaf Italian bread
1 small can black olives
1 small can pimento-stuffed green olives
1 can anchovy fillets
1 package green spinach noodles
1 jar grated Romano cheese
1 bottle Italian dressing
1 pint spumoni or biscuit tortoni
1 bottle dry Italian white wine such as Orvieto or Soave
1 bottle sweet vermouth
1 bottle Marsala

1 PRELIMINARIES

Chill the wine in refrigerator.

Wash, drain, and dry salad greens. Use a few lettuce leaves to line a flat platter, and arrange on it salami slices, prosciutto slices curled into rolls or cornet shapes, green onions, black and green olives, anchovy fillets, and cherry tomatoes. Group to contrast colors and textures. Cover with plastic wrap, and refrigerate. Tear the rest of the salad greens into bite-size pieces, put in a salad bowl, and chill in the refrigerator.

2 PREPARING THE MAIN DISH

INGREDIENTS:

4 veal cutlets, cut thin and pounded flat (by your butcher if he's friendly)
1 clove garlic
$\frac{1}{2}$ c. fine dry bread crumbs
$\frac{1}{4}$ c. chopped chives
1 beaten egg
2 tbsp. flour
$\frac{1}{4}$ c. olive oil
Salt, pepper
$\frac{1}{2}$ c. Marsala

METHOD:

Grate garlic into the bread crumbs, sprinkle in the chives, and mix well. Dip scaloppine pieces into flour, then egg, then bread crumbs; dip again into egg, and once more into bread crumbs. Put aside on waxed paper to set and dry the coating.

Cook the spinach noodles in boiling water. Drain when just barely tender, add 2 tbsp. butter and 3 tbsp. grated Romano cheese.

While noodles are cooking, melt butter in a large skillet over moderate heat, and add olive oil. When well heated, fry scaloppine until golden brown on each side, about 3 minutes per side. Do not overcook. Sprinkle with salt and pepper, then pour Marsala into one side of the pan and swirl it around. Place scaloppine on hot serving platter, and keep warm until serving time.

Warm and crisp the Italian bread wrapped in foil in a 400° oven for 10 minutes.

Add 3–4 tbsp. butter and 3 tbsp. grated cheese to drained noodles, and toss them well.

3 SERVING THE DINNER

Pour 2–3 jiggers of sweet vermouth over ice cubes in large wineglasses. Add a twist of lemon and a splash of club soda.

Bring out the antipasto platter to accompany cocktails.

For the main course, serve scaloppine with hot Marsala-butter sauce poured over them, accompanied by spinach noodles. Add 3–4 tbsp. Italian dressing to green salad, and mix at the dinner table. Serve a basket of hot Italian bread chunks. Pour the wine.

Dessert: spumoni or biscuit tortoni, followed by espresso.

DINNER NUMBER 38
SERVES FOUR

Cook-Ahead. Prepare the main dish in the morning, evening, or even the day before, and heat at serving time.

MENU

MARGARITA

RAW VEGETABLE BITS

PAELLA
GREEN SALAD
HOT FRENCH BREAD

SANGRIA

GUAVA PASTE AND CREAM CHEESE WITH CRACKERS

MARKETING LIST
4 whole chicken breasts split in half (8 pieces)
2 slices Italian salami (approximately 2 oz.)
10 or 12 clams or mussels in the shell or 1 7½-oz. can drained whole or minced clams
8 large raw shrimps
1 lb. onions
1 head lettuce or romaine
1 head curly chicory or escarole
1 bunch watercress
1 small cauliflower
1 bunch radishes
1 cucumber
1 small box cherry tomatoes
1 bunch fennel or celery
1 package frozen peas
1 3-oz. jar sliced red pimento
2 cans chicken broth
1 package rice (white, long grain, not instant)
1 loaf French bread
1 box guava paste
1 box plain, unsalted crackers
1 8-oz. carton sour cream
1 large cream cheese
¼ lb. aged (firm) Romano or Parmesan cheese
1 bottle tequila
2 bottles Sangria or dry white wine
1 pint bottle Triple Sec

1 THE DAY BEFORE: PREPARING THE MAIN DISH

INGREDIENTS:

1 onion, chopped
¼ c. olive oil
8 pieces chicken
1¼ c. uncooked long-grain rice
1½ cans chicken broth (or make it from bouillon cubes)
1 clove garlic, crushed
¼ tsp. shredded saffron or ⅛ tsp. powdered

2 slices salami, cut in slivers
10 or 12 scrubbed clams or mussels in the shell or 7-oz. can minced clams, drained
8 large raw shrimps, shelled
½ package frozen peas
1 3-oz. jar sliced red pimento
¼ c. freshly grated Romano or Parmesan cheese

METHOD:

In a heavy ovenproof pot or skillet, sauté onion in olive oil until golden, about 5 minutes. Lift onion out of oil onto a plate. In the same oil, brown the pieces of chicken for 5 minutes; then remove from pan, and set aside with the onions. Put rice in the pot, adding a little more oil if necessary. Cook, stirring, for 5 minutes or until golden. In a separate pan, heat the chicken consommé with garlic and saffron.

Put chicken, onions, and slivered salami into the ovenproof pot, add consommé, cover, and bake in a 350° oven until rice is cooked, about 1 hour. Cool a little. Push shrimps and clams or mussels down into paella (if using minced clams, stir them in). Sprinkle frozen peas over the top, cover, and refrigerate.

Chill the white wine overnight.

2 ON SERVING DAY

Remove paella from refrigerator.

Wash, drain, and dry salad greens—lettuce, chicory or escarole, and watercress. Tear into bite-size pieces, put in a salad bowl, and refrigerate.

Prepare the raw vegetable appetizer. Break off several sprigs from the cauliflower, wash carefully in salted water, and

drain. Wash radishes and cherry tomatoes. Wash cucumber, score the peel lengthwise with the prongs of a fork, and cut in ¼-inch slices. Discard coarse outer stalks from fennel or celery, and retain the rest (the hearts). Wash very carefully under running water, and cut into quarters or eighths. Arrange vegetables in groups on a large platter or in a shallow bowl. Mix $\frac{1}{3}$ c. mayonnaise with $\frac{1}{3}$ c. sour cream and 3 tbsp. ketchup; season with crushed garlic (1 clove or more if desired), Worcestershire sauce, and a dash or two of Tabasco. Put in a small bowl in the center of the vegetable platter.

Turn oven to 350°. Heat paella, covered, for about 30 minutes. Before serving, decorate with a lattice pattern of pimento strips, and sprinkle with freshly grated cheese.

While paella is heating, warm and crisp the foil-wrapped French bread in the oven for 10–15 minutes. Arrange on small dessert plates 2 or 3 slices of guava paste, a portion of cream cheese, and a few plain crackers. Both cheese and guava paste have a better flavor and texture if served at room temperature, not chilled.

3 SERVING THE DINNER

Dip rims of cocktail glasses into lemon juice, then into coarse salt, and chill them in the refrigerator or preferably the freezer or freezing compartment. You may use a commercial cocktail mix for the Margaritas, or mix them yourself; for 2 drinks, 3 jiggers tequila, 2 jiggers lemon juice, and 1 jigger Triple Sec. Margaritas are best if shaken or blended with *crushed* ice. Accompany cocktails with raw vegetables and dipping sauce.

For the main course, serve paella and a basket of French bread cut in chunks. Pour 4–5 tablespoons of dressing over the green salad, and mix at the table.

Pour Sangria or white wine.

Dessert: guava and cream cheese with crackers.

DINNER NUMBER 39

SERVES TWO

*Cook-Ahead. Prepare the main dish the morning,
evening, or even the day before, and heat at serving time.*

SUPPLY CHECKLIST

Check your supply shelf for the following; if
missing any item, add to marketing list:

Egg (1)
Butter ($\frac{1}{2}$ lb.)
French or Italian dressing
Parsley
Salt, pepper
Whiskey (blended, Scotch, or
          bourbon)
Sugar
Orange (1)

MARKETING LIST

1 broiler chicken, split in half
1 lb. tomatoes
$\frac{1}{4}$ lb. mushrooms
1 package frozen artichoke hearts
2 lemons
1 package heat-and-serve butter-
          flake rolls
1 package medium noodles
1 can pâté de foie
1 package melba toast rounds
1 pint lime sherbet
$\frac{1}{2}$ pint heavy cream
1 bottle Beaujolais
$\frac{1}{2}$ bottle California port wine (red)
$\frac{1}{2}$ bottle brandy, California or French

MENU

WHISKEY SOUR

CHILLED PÂTÉ

FRENCH CHICKEN
BUTTERED NOODLES
COOKED ARTICHOKE HEARTS
TOMATO SALAD
BUTTERFLAKE ROLLS

BEAUJOLAIS

LIME SHERBET

1 THE DAY BEFORE: PREPARING THE MAIN DISH

INGREDIENTS:

1 broiler chicken, split in half	$\frac{1}{2}$ c. heavy cream
Salt, pepper	3 tbsp. port wine
$\frac{1}{2}$ stick plus 3 tbsp. butter	$\frac{1}{4}$ lb. mushrooms, sliced
$\frac{1}{4}$ c. brandy	Parsley

METHOD:

Season chicken pieces with salt and pepper. Sauté chicken, then remove it and hot butter to serving-baking casserole. Pour brandy over, ignite, and let flame die down. Put covered casserole into 350° oven, and bake until almost tender, about $\frac{3}{4}$ hour. Remove chicken from casserole, add cream and port wine, stirring and cooking gently on top of stove over low heat to make a sauce. Replace chicken; allow to cool. Sauté sliced mushrooms in 3 tbsp. butter for 5 minutes, then add to casserole. Cover and refrigerate.

2 ON SERVING DAY

Chill the pâté in the refrigerator.

Cool the wine; it should not be icy cold—1 or 2 hours in the refrigerator is enough.

Hard-boil one egg, cool, and shell.

Take the chicken casserole out of the refrigerator, and let it come to room temperature. Bake, covered, in preheated 350° oven for 15–20 minutes. While it is heating, cook the noodles and the artichoke hearts.

Wash and slice the tomatoes. Arrange in a shallow bowl or on a platter, sprinkle with French or Italian dressing, and add the finely chopped hard-boiled egg on top. Chill until serving time.

Heat rolls in oven.

3 SERVING THE DINNER

Make two whiskey sours, using 4 jiggers whiskey, juice of 1 lemon, and sugar to your guest's own taste. Shake well with ice, and serve in chilled glasses. Garnish with orange section. Serve with chilled pâté and melba toast rounds as appetizer.

For the main course, serve chicken in its baking casserole, along with buttered noodles and artichoke hearts. Use parsley as garnish. Serve tomato salad, and pass a basket of hot rolls.

Dessert: lime sherbet.

DINNER NUMBER 40

SERVES FOUR

*Cook-Ahead. Prepare the main dish the morning,
evening, or even the day before, and heat at serving time.*

MENU

VODKA GIBSON

CUCUMBER RAITA

LAMB CURRY
FLUFFY WHITE RICE, SIDE DISHES
ORANGE-ONION SALAD

BEER

LEMON SHERBET

SUPPLY CHECKLIST

Check your supply shelf for the following; if
missing any item, add to marketing list:

Onion (1)
Eggs (2)
Butter
Olive oil
Flour
Garlic
Bay leaves, cinnamon sticks, cloves
Turmeric, cumin, cardamom seeds
Curry powder, paprika, salt, pepper
Lemon (1)
Vodka
Cocktail onions
Dry vermouth

MARKETING LIST

2 lbs. boned lamb shoulder, cut in
    1-inch cubes
1½ lb. cooking onions
1 piece (2 or 3 oz.) fresh stem ginger
1 green pepper
1 tomato
1 cucumber
1 green pear
2 large, thin-skinned oranges
1 8-oz. carton plain yogurt (not
    sweetened or flavored)
2 cans clear chicken broth
1 package rice (long grain, white,
    not instant)
1 package unsweetened grated
    coconut
1 quart lemon sherbet
1 jar chutney
1 jar watermelon pickles
1 package white raisins
1 package cashews
¼ lb. shelled pine nuts
1 or 2 six-packs beer (choose a
    light, dry beer)

1 THE DAY BEFORE: PREPARING THE MAIN DISH

INGREDIENTS:

2 lbs. boned lamb, in 1-inch cubes	1 tsp. salt
$\frac{1}{4}$ c. flour	$\frac{1}{2}$ tsp. pepper
6 tbsp. butter	2 tsp. paprika
2 tbsp. curry powder	$\frac{1}{4}$ tsp. grated lemon peel
$\frac{1}{2}$ tsp. cumin, crushed	1 slice $\frac{1}{2}$-inch-thick fresh ginger
$\frac{1}{2}$ tsp. cardamom seeds, crushed	4 small cooking onions, peeled
2 cloves	$\frac{1}{2}$ c. white raisins
1 small piece stick cinnamon	$\frac{1}{2}$ c. shelled pine nuts
2 c. chicken broth	1 green pepper, cut into 1 inch squares
1 bay leaf	1 tomato, cut in eighths
$\frac{1}{4}$ tsp. turmeric	1 green pear

METHOD:

It is best to buy spices such as cloves, cumin, cardamom, etc., whole rather than ground. They have more flavor, and stay fresh longer. Before using, they should be pounded fine with a small pestle and mortar, or crushed with a hammer. (Discard outer covering of cardamom.)

Coat meat with flour, and sauté in 4 tbsp. hot butter in a large casserole. In another pan, melt 2 tbsp. butter, add curry powder, and stir; add pounded cloves, cinnamon stick, cumin seed, and cardamom seeds. Add turmeric, and fry gently for a few minutes. Add chicken broth, bay leaf, salt, pepper, paprika, grated lemon rind, and grated or finely minced fresh ginger. Simmer for 2 minutes, then pour over meat. Add peeled onions, raisins, pine nuts, green pepper, and tomato. Cook over medium heat for 2 hours or until tender. Cover and refrigerate overnight. Put beer in refrigerator to chill.

2 ON SERVING DAY

Prepare side dishes for curry. Hardboil 2 eggs. Cool and shell, chop them coarsely, and put in a small bowl. Fill the other bowls with chutney, watermelon pickles, chopped cashews, and coconut. If you can only find the sweetened kind of coconut, rinse it under running water, drain, pat dry; toast slightly in oven.

Make the appetizer as follows: Drain the yogurt in a fine strainer; it must not be too runny. Peel the cucumber, slice lengthwise in quarters, and remove seeds and soft center section. Dice and mix with yogurt. Season with 1 clove garlic, very finely chopped or put through a garlic press. If desired, 1 tbsp. of chopped green onion, parsley, or cilantro (Chinese parsley) may also be added. Chill in refrigerator.

Warm curry over medium heat for 15 minutes. Peel and core the pear, then slice into eighths. Add to curry, and cook for 10 minutes more. While curry is heat-ing, cook 1½ c. rice in boiling salted water according to package directions. Fluff with a fork, and keep warm until serving time. While rice and curry are cooking, peel the oranges, taking off all white pith as well as outer skins. Slice across in ½-inch rings, arrange in a shallow dish, and cover with rings of very thinly sliced onion (white or red). Sprinkle with a little oil and a grat-ing of black pepper. Refrigerate till serving.

3 SERVING THE DINNER

Chill cocktail glasses. Mix vodka Gibsons, or use a commercial premixed cocktail product. For two drinks, the usual recipe, if you want to do it yourself, is 5 jiggers (nearly 8 oz.) vodka to 1 jigger dry vermouth, stirred well with ice. Serve in chilled glasses with a pearl onion in each, with cucumber raita as an appetizer, accompanied by corn chips or small sec-tions of crisped poppadum to spoon it out.

For the main course, serve lamb curry along with fluffy rice and side dishes. Bring out the orange-onion salad. Bread is not usually served with a curry, but if you buy poppadums for the dip, you can offer some of them with the main course. They should be crisped by frying or toasting in the oven.

Pour cold beer in tall glasses.

Dessert: lemon sherbet.

DINNER NUMBER 41

SERVES FOUR

*Cook-Ahead. Prepare the main dish the morning,
evening, or even the day before, and heat at serving time.*

MENU

MANHATTAN

SALTED AND SPICED NUTS

BLANQUETTE DE VEAU
FLUFFY RICE, SPINACH
AND WATERCRESS SALAD
CRISP HARD ROLLS

MUSCADET OR SANCERRE

FRESH FRUIT COMPOTE

SUPPLY CHECKLIST

Check your supply shelf for the following; if
missing any item, add to marketing list:

Butter
Flour
Egg (1)
Lemon (1)
Garlic
Bay leaf
Peppercorns
Whiskey
Vermouth, dry and sweet

MARKETING LIST

2 lbs. veal, cut in cubes as for stew
1 bunch celery
$\frac{1}{2}$ lb. mushrooms
$1\frac{1}{2}$ lbs. small onions (12)
1 bunch carrots
1 bunch parsley
Ripe fresh fruit for compote, such
     as peaches (2), pears (2), ber-
     ries (small basket)
1 package or 1 lb. fresh young
     spinach
1 bunch watercress
1 package frozen melon balls
1 small carton heavy cream
1 package rice (white, long grain,
     not instant)
1 package hard French rolls, bake-
     and-serve
1 bottle Thousand Island dressing
Salted, spiced, or garlic-flavored
     nuts (almonds, cashews, maca-
     damias, peanuts)
2 bottles Loire-Valley dry white wine,
     such as Muscadet or Sancerre,
     or an equivalent California
     Riesling
1 small bottle liqueur

1 THE DAY BEFORE: PREPARING THE MAIN DISH

INGREDIENTS:

2 lbs. lean veal, preferably from the leg, cut in cubes
1 tsp. salt
2 stalks celery
1 bay leaf
8 peppercorns
1 clove garlic
8 small carrots, cut in 2-inch lengths

12 small white onions, peeled
3 tbsp. butter
3 tbsp. flour
$\frac{1}{2}$ c. plus 2 tbsp. heavy cream
1 egg yolk
$\frac{1}{2}$ lb. mushrooms
Juice of $\frac{1}{2}$ lemon
Chopped parsley

METHOD:

Put veal pieces in a saucepan, and cover with cold water. Bring to a boil, cook 5 minutes, then pour off water. Cover again with fresh cold water. Add salt, celery, bay leaf, peppercorns, and garlic, and cook slowly over low flame for 1 hour. Add carrots and onions, and cook for $\frac{1}{2}$ hour longer, or until meat is tender.

Skim meat, carrots, and onions out of liquid, and put them in a covered dish. Refrigerate. Reduce the cooking liquid by boiling over high heat until it measures $1\frac{1}{2}$ c. (about half the original amount). Strain into a clean pan or bowl.

In a small pan, melt the butter, stir in the flour, and cook slowly for 1 or 2 minutes. Dilute with the reduced cooking liquid, and cook, stirring with a small whisk, until it is smooth and thickened. Beat the egg yolk with $\frac{1}{2}$ c. cream. Add 2–3 tbsp. of the hot sauce to the egg-cream mixture, and stir it slowly into the sauce (away from the heat). Return to a low flame, and continue stirring until the sauce is blended and thickened. It must *not* boil, or it will curdle. Set aside to cool.

Cook mushroom caps in $\frac{1}{2}$ c. salted water with the juice of $\frac{1}{2}$ lemon for 5 minutes. Add drained mushrooms to the meat and vegetables in the casserole. Add mushroom cooking liquid to sauce in the pan. Stir well, and float 2 tbsp. cream over the top to prevent it from forming a skin. Cover and refrigerate.

2 ON SERVING DAY

Chill the white wine.

Prepare fruit compote. Thaw melon balls, and add to them small sections of fresh peach and pear and a few berries cut in half. If fresh fruit is not available, canned peach sections or pineapple may be used instead. Sprinkle each portion with 1–2 tsp. liqueur. (Kirsch, Cointreau, Curaçao, or other fruit-flavored liqueurs are best.) Refrigerate.

Wash and pick over watercress, dividing into small sprigs and discarding any tough stems. Choose only the small, pale green spinach leaves, and wash very carefully (change the water two or three times—spinach is often very sandy). The rest of the spinach can be used for another meal. Arrange watercress and spinach in a salad bowl, and refrigerate.

Cook 1½ c. rice according to package directions.

Take the veal-vegetable mixture and the sauce out of the refrigerator. Stir the sauce well, and pour over all the other ingredients. Heat very gently until at simmering point over a very low flame or in a 250° oven. Allow 15–20 minutes for heating, because it cannot be hurried; if the sauce boils, it will curdle. Chop 2 tbsp. parsley for a garnish.

Heat and crisp hard rolls according to package directions.

3 SERVING THE DINNER

Make two Manhattan cocktails, using a premix if you wish. If you prefer to do it yourself, stir 4 jiggers whiskey, 1 jigger dry vermouth, and 1 jigger sweet vermouth with ice cubes. Serve on the rocks or straight up in chilled glasses. Put the salted and spiced nuts in a small dish as an accompaniment to the cocktails.

For the main course, sprinkle parsley over the blanquette, and serve in its casserole, accompanied by a bowl of fluffy rice. Serve the watercress-spinach salad, tossed with 4–5 tbsp. of Thousand Island dressing. Wrap hot rolls in a napkin and put in basket. Pour the white wine.

Dessert: fresh fruit compote.

DINNER NUMBER 42

SERVES FOUR

*Cook-Ahead. Prepare the main dish the morning,
evening, or even the day before, and heat at serving time.*

SUPPLY CHECKLIST

Check your supply shelf for the following; if
missing any item, add to marketing list:

Butter (½ stick)
Eggs (2)
Plain unflavored gelatin
Dried thyme
Garlic
Worcestershire sauce
Salt, pepper
Mayonnaise
Dry vermouth
Gin

MARKETING LIST

6 large slices rare roast beef, ¼-inch
    thick (from delicatessen)
1 green pepper
1 bunch carrots
1 bunch watercress
1 head lettuce
1 package frozen peas
1 package frozen green beans
1 can small new potatoes
2 cans lobster bisque or 2 cans
    frozen shrimp soup
2 cans consommé
1 loaf French bread
1 frozen strawberry cheesecake
2 bottles rosé wine, French or
    California

MENU

DRY MARTINI

LOBSTER BISQUE

BEEF IN ASPIC
MIMOSA SALAD
HOT GARLIC BREAD

CHILLED ROSÉ

STRAWBERRY CHEESECAKE

1 THE DAY BEFORE: PREPARING THE MAIN DISH

Wash 4 or 5 large carrots, and scrape or peel thinly. Cook in boiling salted water to cover them until just tender. Drain and cool. Cook ½ package of green beans and ½ package green peas according to directions. Drain and chill. Hard-boil 2 eggs (10 minutes); cool, shell, and chill.

INGREDIENTS:

6 slices rare roast beef
Salt, pepper, thyme
2 10½ oz. cans consomme
2 envelopes unflavored gelatin
½ c. cold water

1 tsp. Worcestershire sauce
1 or 2 carrots, cooked and chilled
Strips of green pepper
Watercress

METHOD:

Arrange roast beef slices, overlapping, in shallow serving dish. Season to taste with salt, pepper, and thyme. Make an aspic by heating consommé with 1½ soup cans of water.

Soften gelatin in ½ c. water for 5 minutes; then add to hot consommé. Stir to dissolve. Add Worcestershire sauce. Pour a small quantity of liquid aspic over beef slices. Arrange slices of carrot and strips of green pepper in a decorative pattern over the beef. Chill in refrigerator until set; then add another coating of the aspic, spooning it carefully over the slices of beef so you don't disarrange the garnish. Chill again. If there is any aspic left over, chill it in a shallow dish until firmly set, and at serving time, dice and use it as an extra garnish.

2 ON SERVING DAY

Prepare the mimosa salad: Drain canned potatoes, and cube enough to make ½–⅓ cup. Dice the other cooked carrots, including any pieces left from garnishing the beef aspic. Mix carrots, potatoes, cooked green peas, and green beans with about ½ c. mayonnaise. Season with additional salt, pepper, and a dash of Worcestershire sauce. Wash, drain, and pat dry enough lettuce leaves to line a salad bowl. On the lettuce bed, arrange the mixed vegetable salad. Chop the whites of the hard-boiled eggs, and scatter over the vegetable salad; on top of this, sprinkle the egg yolks pushed through a sieve or strainer. Refrigerate until serving.

Wash and trim 12 sprigs of watercress for garnish. Heat soup.

Brush French bread with ½ stick melted butter seasoned with 1 or 2 cloves of crushed garlic. Heat until crisp wrapped in foil in a 400° oven (about 10 minutes).

3 SERVING THE DINNER

Chill cocktail glasses. Mix martinis, using 5 parts gin to 1 part dry vermouth for each drink, stirred well with ice (or use a premix if you prefer). Serve in chilled glasses with a cocktail olive or a twist of lemon. Make a fresh batch when you want refills.

Serve hot lobster bisque or shrimp soup in cups or small bowls.

For the main course, take beef aspic out of the refrigerator (at the very last minute), and garnish with watercress sprigs (they will wilt if you put them on ahead of time) and any extra aspic, finely chopped. Serve beef aspic, accompanied by the mimosa salad and hot garlic bread. Pour chilled rosé wine.

Dessert: strawberry cheesecake.

DINNER NUMBER 43

SERVES FOUR

Cook-Ahead. Prepare the main dish the morning, evening, or even the day before, and heat at serving time.

MENU

OLD-FASHIONED

PÂTÉ

CHICKEN GUILLERMO
POTATO PUFFS
MIXED GREEN SALAD
HOT FRENCH BREAD

RIESLING

RASPBERRY SHERBET

1 THE DAY BEFORE: PREPARING THE MAIN DISH

INGREDIENTS:
2 chicken breasts (4 pieces) | **1 stick butter**
2 chicken legs (4 pieces) | **3–4 mild onions, sliced**

METHOD:

Melt half of butter in large, flameproof casserole. Put in enough onion slices to make a layer about 1½ inches deep. Cook over low heat for about 5 minutes, until golden. Melt remaining butter in a large skillet, and cook pieces of chicken until golden brown; it is better to do them in two batches than to crowd them. Allow about 10 minutes cooking time for breast portions, turning once, and slightly longer for legs. Arrange browned chicken on top of sautéd onions, and add any butter left in the skillet. Cover casserole, and cook in a 300° oven until chicken is tender and the onions are reduced to a purée (about 1 hour). Refrigerate in casserole.

2 ON SERVING DAY

Chill the Riesling wine.

Wash, drain, and dry salad greens. Tear into bite-size pieces, and put into a large salad bowl. Refrigerate until serving.

Heat potato puffs according to package directions. Wrap French bread in foil and heat in the same oven for ten minutes.

Reheat chicken casserole gently over very low flame, 15–20 minutes.

3 SERVING THE DINNER

Chill old-fashioned glasses. Put one lump of sugar into each, and sprinkle with a dash of Angostura bitters. Add ice cubes and an orange slice to each, then fill with whiskey. Serve drinks with stirrers or straws in the glasses.

Accompany drinks with pâté and crackers for an appetizer.

For the main course, pour about ¼ c. preferred dressing over salad; toss and mix at the dinner table. Serve chicken Guillermo and hot French bread.

Pour the wine.

Dessert: raspberry sherbet.

DINNER NUMBER 44

SERVES FOUR

Cook-Ahead. Prepare the main dish the morning,
evening, or even the day before, and heat at serving time.

MENU

DAIQUIRI

SHERRIED CONSOMMÉ

COLD POACHED SALMON STEAK
BUTTERED NEW POTATOES
WILTED CUCUMBER SALAD
SESAME SEED ROLLS

WHITE BURGUNDY

FRESH FRUIT PLATTER

1 THE DAY BEFORE: PREPARING THE MAIN DISH

INGREDIENTS:

$\frac{1}{2}$ c. white wine	1 tsp. salt
2 quarts water	$\frac{1}{2}$ bay leaf
4 salmon steaks	2 or 3 sprigs parsley
$\frac{1}{2}$ large carrot, sliced	Watercress for garnish
$\frac{1}{2}$ large onion, cut up	1 large square cheesecloth to wrap fish
2 cloves	(this may be available in the super-
3 peppercorns	market; if not, check the hardware
1 stalk celery, sliced	or dime store)

METHOD:

In a large deep pan or kettle, prepare the broth for cooking the fish (this is called a court bouillon): Put in 2 quarts water, $\frac{1}{2}$ c. wine; add carrot, onion, celery, parsley, salt, peppercorns, cloves, bay leaf, and salt. Bring to the boil, and simmer for 10 minutes. Pack salmon slices side by side, as if they were one large piece, and wrap in a large square of cheesecloth. Tie the corners together in a loose knot. Lower gently into simmering broth, and cook on a low heat, barely simmering for 15–20 minutes, about 10 minutes per pound. Lift out of liquid with a pair of tongs, drain, and set aside to cool. Unwrap, separate steaks, and carefully peel off skin. Arrange side by side on serving dish. Cover with plastic wrap, and refrigerate. Throw away skin, cheesecloth, and the broth (unless you are ambitious and want to use the broth to make chowder or bisque the next day!)

Refrigerate the white wine.

2 ON SERVING DAY

Prepare the cucumber salad as follows: Peel cucumber, and slice it. Put slices in a bowl, sprinkling each layer quite heavily with salt. Refrigerate for at least 1 hour.

Arrange fruit platter, using fresh green leaves as a base if available. Magnolia leaves are wonderful and do not wilt, but caladium, fern, or other leaves add to the beauty of the arrangement. Refrigerate until serving time.

Wash watercress for garnishing the salmon, and fill four tiny bowls or Chinese pottery soup spoons with mayonnaise. Drain canned new potatoes, and heat gently with butter, or cook frozen new potatoes according to directions. Heat sesame-seed rolls.

Take sliced cucumber out of refrigerator. Put in a colander or strainer, and rinse under cold running water, squeezing out water and salt. Put back in bowl, sprinkle with 1 tbsp. powdered sugar, a dash of pepper, and 3–4 tbsp. wine vinegar. Mix well, and if desired, sprinkle with $\frac{1}{4}$ tsp. caraway seeds. Refrigerate until serving.

Heat $1\frac{1}{2}$ cans consommé with $1\frac{1}{2}$ cans water, and add $\frac{1}{4}$ c. sherry. Keep warm until serving time.

3 SERVING THE DINNER

Mix the Daiquiris, using a blender if you have one. For two drinks, mix 4 jiggers light rum, 2 tbsp. fresh lime juice, and 4 tsp. superfine sugar. Put 2 c. shaved or crushed ice in blender, add rum and lime mixture, and blend until snowlike. Serve in chilled glasses with a straw. If you don't have a blender, shake the same mixture with ice cubes, and strain into glasses.

For the main course, garnish cold salmon platter with watercress and lemon quarters, and accompany by bowls or spoons of mayonnaise. Serve new potatoes, cucumber salad, and hot sesame seed rolls.

Pour the white wine.

Dessert: platter of assorted fruit.

DINNER NUMBER 45

SERVES FOUR

Cook-Ahead. Prepare the main dish the morning, evening, or even the day before, and heat at serving time.

SUPPLY CHECKLIST

Check your supply shelf for the following; if missing any item, add to marketing list:

Lemon (1)
Dried thyme or sage
Flour
Oil
Salt, pepper
Rose's lime juice (sweetened) or
    grenadine
Club soda

MARKETING LIST

8 small pork chops (2–2½ lbs.)
16–20 cooked shrimp
Salad greens: lettuce, chicory, water-
    cress
1 lb. onions
2 packages frozen baby lima beans
1 small can mandarin orange sections
1 package rice (white, long grain)
1 package bake-and-serve hard rolls
1 bottle shrimp cocktail sauce
1 chocolate chiffon pie, frozen or
    from bakery
1 bottle cider (hard cider if obtain-
    able)
1 bottle vodka
2 bottles California Zinfandel
1 bottle applejack or Calvados
    (optional)

MENU

JACK ROSE

SHRIMP COCKTAIL

PORK CHOPS BORRACHO
FLUFFY RICE, GREEN SALAD
HARD FRENCH ROLLS

CALIFORNIA ZINFANDEL

CHOCOLATE CHIFFON PIE

1 THE DAY BEFORE: PREPARING THE MAIN DISH

INGREDIENTS:

8 pork chops
Flour, salt, pepper
2 packages frozen baby lima beans
2 medium onions, sliced thin

1 tsp. thyme or a pinch of sage
1 c. cider
$\frac{1}{4}$ c. applejack or Calvados (optional)

METHOD:

Heat a large heavy skillet, and rub with the fat edge of one chop to grease. Dip chops into flour seasoned with salt and pepper. Sauté meat until brown, about 7 minutes for each side. Transfer chops to a large baking dish, and cover with the lima beans (bang the packages against the edge of the sink to break them up) and the onion slices. Season with thyme or sage. Pour cider into skillet, and heat for 1 or 2 minutes, scraping the bottom of the pan to get up all the brown bits. Then pour over chops in the baking dish. Cover with foil, and bake 1 hour at 350°. Add more cider if dish gets dry. Cool and refrigerate.

2 ON SERVING DAY

Chill the wine. Take casserole out of refrigerator and let come to room temperature. Wash, drain, and dry salad greens. Use a few small lettuce leaves to line bowls or small plates on which you plan to serve the shrimp cocktail. Arrange 4–5 peeled shrimps in each bowl. Add about 2 tbsp. cocktail sauce to each, and chill till serving time.

Tear enough of the remaining salad greens for four good-sized portions into bite-size pieces; put into salad bowl and refrigerate.

Drain mandarin orange sections, saving some of the juice. Make a dressing for the salad by shaking in a screw-top jar 4 tbsp. oil, 1 tbsp. mandarin juice, 1 tbsp. lemon juice, $\frac{1}{2}$ tsp. salt, and $\frac{1}{4}$ tsp. black pepper. Shake well and chill.

Cook $1\frac{1}{2}$ cups rice according to .package directions.

Pour applejack or Calvados (if available) over pork chops, and heat in 350° oven for about 20 minutes.

While casserole is heating, warm hard rolls.

3 SERVING
THE DINNER

If you buy applejack or Calvados specially for the main dish, you may want to use some of it to make an unusual and delicious cocktail, a Jack Rose. Shake with ice cubes 3 jiggers applejack, 1 jigger grenadine, and the juice of $1\frac{1}{2}$ limes. Strain into chilled glasses. If you skip the applejack as an ingredient for the main dish, then vodka gimlets are suggested. For these, stir with ice 3 parts gin to 1 part Rose's lime juice; strain into glasses, and add a splash of club soda.

After the drinks, serve shrimp cocktails. Arrange mandarin sections over salad greens, and pour well-shaken dressing over; toss and mix at the dinner table.

For the main course serve pork chops Borracho, with rice and salad.

Pour the wine.

Dessert: chocolate chiffon pie.

DINNER NUMBER 46

SERVES FOUR TO SIX

Cook-Ahead. Prepare the main dish the morning, evening, or even the day before, and heat at serving time.

MENU

ROB ROY

ANTIPASTO

MEATBALL AND EGGPLANT CASSEROLE
GREEN SALAD
HOT GARLIC BREAD

CHIANTI

BISCUIT TORTONI

SUPPLY CHECKLIST

Check your supply shelf for the following; if missing any item, add to marketing list:

Oil ($1\frac{1}{4}$ c.)
Egg (1)
Butter, $\frac{1}{2}$ stick
Onion (1)
Garlic
Cornstarch
Oregano
Ground allspice
Salt, pepper
Flour
Scotch whiskey
Sweet vermouth
Dry vermouth

MARKETING LIST

$1\frac{1}{2}$ lbs. chuck steak, put *twice* through meat grinder
$\frac{1}{4}$ lb. thinly sliced Cotto salami
6 slices mortadella sausage
$\frac{1}{4}$ lb. prosciutto
$\frac{1}{4}$ lb. sliced provolone cheese
⎫ from delicatessen counter ⎬
Salad greens, assorted; including lettuce, escarole, chicory and rugala, if available
1 small box cherry tomatoes
1 medium eggplant
1 bunch parsley or watercress
1 bunch green onions
1 8-oz. package mozzarella cheese
2 15-oz. cans tomato sauce
1 can anchovy fillets, flat or curled
1 jar small Italian peppers (pepperoncini)
1 can black olives
1 bottle Italian dressing
1 package seasoned bread crumbs
1 large or 2 small loaves Italian bread
$\frac{1}{2}$ pint light cream
1 quart biscuit tortoni
2 bottles Chianti or Bardolino

1 THE DAY BEFORE: PREPARING THE MAIN DISH

INGREDIENTS:

1½ **lbs. ground chuck steak**	¼ **c. oil for frying meatballs**
¾ **c. seasoned bread crumbs**	1 **medium-size eggplant**
1 **small onion, chopped fine**	⅓ **c. flour**
¾ **tsp. cornstarch**	¼ **tsp. salt**
1 **egg, beaten**	½ **to 1 c. olive oil**
¾ **c. light cream**	1 **8-oz. mozzarella cheese, shredded**
¾ **tsp. salt**	2 **15-oz. cans tomato sauce**
Dash allspice	½ **tsp. oregano**

METHOD:

Mix first 8 ingredients together. Roll and press by hand into balls about 1½ inches in diameter. Heat ¼ c. oil in skillet, and brown the meatballs all over, shaking the pan to color them evenly.

Slice eggplant into ½-inch slices. Dip in flour mixed with salt. Sauté a few slices at a time in hot oil in a large skillet. (Start off with ¼ c. oil, and add more as necessary.)

Cook till golden brown, 4–5 minutes each side. In a large, square casserole or baking pan, arrange a layer of half the eggplant slices; on top put half the meat balls, tomato sauce, and cheese. Sprinkle with ¼ tsp. oregano, and repeat the layers, using the remainder of the ingredients. Cover with plastic wrap, and refrigerate.

2 ON SERVING DAY

Take casserole out of the refrigerator, and allow to come to room temperature (about 1 hour). Meanwhile arrange antipasto in a large platter or on a lazy Susan, using salami, mortadella, and prosciutto folded into rolls or cornet shapes, small slices or fingers of provolone, cherry tomatoes, black olives, Italian peppers, anchovy curls or fillets, a few washed and trimmed green onions, and sprigs of parsley, chicory, or watercress to garnish. Keep cool until serving time.

Wash salad greens. Drain, dry, and tear into bite-size pieces. Put into a large salad bowl and refrigerate.

Heat oven to 350°, and bake meatball-eggplant casserole, uncovered, for approximately 1 hour, until cheese is melted and sauce bubbly.

Season ½ stick melted butter with

1 clove crushed garlic and brush over top and sides of French bread, wrapped in foil, and heat in oven until crisp (approximately 10–15 minutes).

3 SERVING THE DINNER

Mix Rob Roy cocktails, using a premix if you prefer. If you'd sooner do it yourself, stir with ice in a pitcher 1 jigger Scotch whiskey and $\frac{1}{3}$ jigger each of sweet and dry vermouth plus a dash of Angostura bitters for each person. Serve straight or on the rocks with a twist of lemon peel. (For six people you'd need 6 jiggers Scotch, 2 of sweet vermouth, and 2 of dry.) Serve antipasto platter as appetizer.

For the main course, keep meatball and eggplant casserole bubbling hot; have warmed plates. Pour 6–8 tbsp. dressing on the salad, and mix at the dinner table. Serve garlic bread sliced into chunks.

Pour Chianti or Bardolino, using good-size wineglasses.

Dessert: biscuit tortoni.

CHAPTER 5

BRUNCH MENUS

Brunch is a modern invention . . . a bit *more* than breakfast, but not quite lunch. You can play it as close to either as you like, because there are no unbreakable rules.

This meal, *usually* served from eleven A.M. to two P.M., can start with a cocktail, proceed to an appetizer, main course and dessert. It *may* be accompanied by wine; but wine isn't necessary. If you prefer, omit the cocktails and wine, and serve cold, fresh juice with lots of hot, fresh coffee. If your party is to be Sunday morning after a big Saturday night, the coffee tactic may make you *more* popular than any expertise with a cocktail shaker.

The vital ingredients for a successful brunch are friendly informality plus good food. It's a meal for *friends,* not the repayment of a duty invitation. Start the party at an hour that suits you best; even if guests linger so long you have to make a fourth pot of coffee, you'll still be finished before six P.M. In fact, brunch could have been invented specially for the working girl! This meal may be served sitting down, as a buffet, or on trays.

A few general guidelines: Most people don't like drinking Scotch or martinis early in the day, not because they're priggish, but because straight hard liquor doesn't taste so nifty so soon after getting out of bed. Vodka drinks (bloody Marys, screwdrivers, bullshots) are good possibilities. Orange, grapefruit, pineapple juice . . . fresh and clean-tasting,

spiked with a fizz (club soda, tonic, bitter lemon) are all excellent; so is a fresh-fruit daiquiri. Perhaps the most glamorous and welcome of all liquids is champagne, alone or combined with orange juice.

The brunch main dish tends to revolve around items like eggs, bacon, sausage, pancakes . . . all those delicious breakfasty treats you don't have time to cook creatively on an ordinary morning. There are supposed to be 365 ways to cook eggs, and so we've chosen *them* as the principal ingredient for more than half our menus. But if you *hate* eggs, and want to skip *all* breakfast menus, borrow a recipe from one of the dinner menus in Chapter 4. If what you crave at Sunday brunch is spaghetti, fried chicken, a hamburger, or even a steak, go right ahead and set a *new* fashion!

There's no obligation to provide dessert at brunch, at least not a conventional one. Sweet rolls, coffee cake, or cinnamon toast are three possibilities, or if everybody seems to be counting calories, consider a beautiful melon or berries. You *may* make brunch into a dessert fantasia by cooking up a big batch of pancakes and offering a dozen different toppings: honey, *real* maple syrup, thawed strawberries, fresh blueberries and sour cream, chocolate or butterscotch fudge, Lyle's Golden Syrup, lingonberries, hot applesauce, ice cream. It does seem that all the most enjoyable things *are* immoral, illegal, or fattening . . . so enjoy!

BRUNCH NUMBER 1

SERVES FOUR

SUPPLY CHECKLIST
Check your supply shelf for the following; if
missing any item, add to marketing list:

Lemon (1)
Lime (1)
Sugar
Flour
Salt, pepper
Coffee
Gin

MARKETING LIST
$\frac{1}{2}$ dozen eggs
$\frac{1}{2}$ lb. Swiss cheese (natural cheese in
    one piece, *not* processed)
$\frac{1}{2}$ lb. bacon
1 quart milk
1 frozen 8-inch pie shell, or piecrust
    mix
1 head lettuce, romaine or escarole
1 bunch watercress
2 oranges
1 small fresh pineapple
1 package shredded coconut
1 bottle preferred salad dressing

MENU

SILVER FIZZ

QUICHE LORRAINE
GREEN SALAD

FRESH ORANGE SLICES
PINEAPPLE CHUNKS
AND SHREDDED COCONUT

CAFÉ AU LAIT

1 PRELIMINARIES

Peel oranges, cutting off all white pith; then slice into rings. Peel pineapple, removing all brown spiny pieces. Cut into thick slices, then into chunks, trimming off hard center core. Mix orange and pineapple, and sprinkle with sugar. Refrigerate.

Wash salad greens, drain, and pat dry. Tear into pieces, put in salad bowl, and chill in refrigerator.

2 PREPARING THE MAIN DISH

INGREDIENTS:

4–6 slices bacon	**1 c. milk**
½ lb. Swiss cheese	**3 eggs**
Dash of salt and pepper	

METHOD:

Heat oven to 325°.

Cook bacon slowly until crisp; then drain. When cool, crumble into pieces. Grate the cheese coarsely, and mix with flour, salt, and pepper. Heat milk. Beat eggs, and slowly add hot milk. Add the grated cheese, and stir well. Sprinkle bacon over the bottom of the unbaked pieshell. Pour over it the cheese-egg-milk mixture, and put into oven to bake for 30–40 minutes. Test with a silver knife; when the quiche is fully cooked, the knife will come out clean.

While the quiche is cooking, prepare good strong coffee, and warm the milk to serve with it. Don't boil the milk, or it will form a skin, which you will have to strain out before serving.

3 SERVING THE BRUNCH

Make the silver fizz, in a blender if possible. Use 2 jiggers gin, the juice of ½ lemon, the juice of ½ lime, 1 tbsp. sugar, and 1 egg white for 2 drinks. Blend with crushed ice until white and frothy. Pour into chilled glasses. If you don't have a blender, shake well in a cocktail shaker and strain into glasses.

After the cocktails, serve the quiche cut into wedges, accompanied by the green salad, tossed and mixed with 3–4 tbsp. salad dressing.

Pour out the café au lait (coffee and hot milk) into large cups or mugs.

Dessert: orange-pineapple slices sprinkled with shredded coconut.

BRUNCH NUMBER 2
SERVES FOUR

SUPPLY CHECKLIST
Check your supply shelf for the following; if missing any item, add to marketing list:

Lemon (1)
Butter (1 stick)
Coffee
Onion (1 medium)
Tabasco
Black pepper
Cinnamon sticks
Poppy seeds
Mustard (mixed, salad, or Dijon-style)
Mayonnaise or salad dressing

MARKETING LIST
$\frac{1}{2}$ lb. bacon
$\frac{1}{2}$ lb. sliced Swiss cheese (natural, *not* processed)
1 long loaf French or Italian bread
1 large or 2 small bunches fennel or celery
1 box cherry tomatoes
1 bunch watercress
1 large can pitted apricots
1 package whole almonds
1 bottle almond extract
1 medium can tomato juice

MENU

SPICED TOMATO JUICE

SPEDINI ALLA ROMANA
FINGER SALAD

BLACK COFFEE

APRICOT-ALMOND COMPOTE

1 PRELIMINARIES

Chill the tomato juice in refrigerator. Wash tomatoes and watercress. Trim off outside leaves of fennel or celery, and cut hearts into quarters or eighths. Arrange vegetables in groups on a platter with a small bowl of mayonnaise or salad dressing in the center.

Drain apricots from syrup. Keep the syrup. Into each apricot, tuck a peeled almond (almonds can be peeled very easily by soaking for a few minutes in boiling water). Arrange in a shallow bowl. Pour apricot syrup into a small pan, and cook over low heat until slightly reduced and thickened. Add $\frac{1}{2}$ tsp. almond extract. Reheat and pour over apricots. Chill.

2 PREPARING THE MAIN DISH

INGREDIENTS:

- 1 loaf French or Italian bread
- 1 stick butter
- $\frac{1}{4}$ c. chopped onion
- 2–3 tbsp. mixed mustard
- 1 tbsp. poppy seeds
- $\frac{1}{2}$ lb. sliced Swiss cheese
- 4 slices bacon, cut in half

METHOD:

Heat oven to 350°.

Trim most of the crust from top and sides of the bread, and slash *almost* to the bottom at 1-inch intervals. Sauté the chopped onion in butter until softened, then stir in mustard and poppy seeds. Spread this mixture between the slashes of the bread.

Insert a slice of cheese in each slash, and arrange the strips of bacon over the top of the loaf. Bake in a 350° oven until the bacon is crisp and the cheese melted (about 5 minutes).

3 SERVING THE BRUNCH

Season chilled tomato juice with Tabasco, lemon juice, and black pepper to taste. Decorate glasses with a semicircle of lemon perched on the edge (put a slash in the middle of the slice so it will balance).

Follow with the hot spedini, the salad platter, and cups of hot black coffee with a cinnamon stick in each. Offer whipped cream to stir into coffee.

Dessert: apricot-almond compote.

BRUNCH NUMBER 3
SERVES FOUR

SUPPLY CHECKLIST
Check your supply shelf for the following; if missing any item, add to marketing list:

Peanut oil
Soy sauce
Worcestershire sauce
Cornstarch
Tea (preferably Chinese)
Vodka
Lemons (2)

MARKETING LIST
1 dozen eggs
$\frac{3}{4}$–1 lb. shrimps, fresh or frozen
1 bunch celery
1 bunch green onions
$\frac{1}{4}$ lb. fresh mushrooms or 1 can
       sliced mushrooms
1 can bean sprouts
2 cans chicken consommé
1 can beef bouillon
1 can chow mein noodles
1 package fortune cookies

MENU

BULLSHOT

EGGS FOO YONG
CHOW MEIN NOODLES

CHINESE TEA

FORTUNE COOKIES

1 PREPARING THE MAIN DISH

INGREDIENTS:

Sauce:
2 cans chicken consomme
2 tbsp. soy sauce
**2 tbsp. cornstarch, blended smoothly
    with a little cold water**

Pancakes:
8 beaten eggs
5 green onions, chopped
½ c. sliced mushrooms
1 c. bean sprouts
½ c. chopped celery
1 c. cooked shrimps, chopped

METHOD:

Combine sauce ingredients, and simmer until clear and thickened. Keep warm over low heat.

Combine pancake ingredients. Heat 2–3 tbsp. peanut oil in a large skillet. Use a large spoon or a ¼-cup measure to portion out the mixture for each pancake; they should be small. Fry the pancakes a few at a time. Turn them to brown on each side. Keep cooked cakes warm in a slow oven (250°) until all are done.

Heat and crisp chow mein noodles in a shallow pan in the oven while pancakes are being cooked.

2 SERVING THE BRUNCH

Make bullshots as follows: Use large old-fashioned glasses (you need something bigger than a regular cocktail glass). Put 2 or 3 ice cubes in each glass. Add 2 jiggers beef bouillon, 1 jigger vodka, 1 tbsp. lemon juice, and a dash of Worcestershire sauce. Cut two stalks of celery in half lengthwise, and use for stirrers.

For the main course, serve three or four pancakes for each portion, with the hot sauce spooned over them. Bring out a bowl of crisp chow mein noodles, and offer cups of hot Chinese tea.

Dessert: fortune cookies.

BRUNCH NUMBER 4

SERVES FOUR

SUPPLY CHECKLIST

Check your supply shelf for the following; if missing any item, add to marketing list:

Butter
Tabasco
Worcestershire sauce
Coffee
Salt, pepper, dried basil
Vodka

MARKETING LIST

1 dozen eggs
4 large tomatoes
Fresh fruit in season, such as pears, grapes, etc.
2 lemons
2 packages frozen creamed spinach
1 jar or tin grated Parmesan cheese
2 or 3 types of cheese, such as Brie, Camembert, Swiss, Crema Danica, Gouda, Monterey Jack, etc.
1 large can tomato juice
1 large loaf French bread

MENU

BLOODY MARY

EGGS FLORENTINE
BROILED TOMATOES
FRENCH BREAD

COFFEE

FRESH FRUIT AND CHEESE

1 PRELIMINARIES

Wash and drain fruit, and arrange on a large platter with the cheese wedges. Cover with plastic wrap, and chill.

2 PREPARING THE MAIN DISH

INGREDIENTS:

2 packages creamed spinach	Tabasco
Butter for greasing baking dish	4 large tomatoes
6 tbsp. grated or shredded Parmesan cheese	Salt, pepper, dried basil
8 eggs	2 tbsp. butter

METHOD:

Heat oven to 350°.

Cook spinach according to package directions. Butter a large, flat baking dish or ovenproof platter, and spread cooked spinach evenly over it. Sprinkle with 4 tbsp. of the Parmesan cheese. With the back of a spoon make 8 evenly spaced hollows in the spinach. Break an egg into each hollow; sprinkle with salt and the remaining Parmesan cheese. Add 1 drop of Tabasco on each egg yolk.

Cut tomatoes in half crosswise.

Place on another baking dish, sprinkle each half with salt, pepper, and a pinch of basil, then dot with butter.

Put the eggs and spinach in the oven at 350°, and place the tomatoes under the broiler. Bake the eggs about 8 minutes, or until they are set, while the tomatoes are broiling.

Brew the coffee. Wrap French bread in foil, and heat in oven until crisp, about 10 minutes.

3 SERVING THE BRUNCH

Make four Bloody Marys by shaking well with ice 4 jiggers vodka, 8 jiggers tomato juice, the juice of 2 lemons (4 tbsp.), and Worcestershire sauce, Tabasco, and freshly ground black pepper to taste.

For the main course, serve eggs Florentine and broiled tomatoes, accompanied by French bread and butter. Pour hot coffee.

Dessert: platter of fruit and cheese.

BRUNCH NUMBER 5
SERVES FOUR

MARKETING LIST
1 dozen eggs
1 lb. onions
1 medium-size green pepper
2 tomatoes
1 quart basket strawberries or 2 packages frozen whole berries
1 bunch parsley
2 thin-skinned oranges
1 can or jar green asparagus tips
1 jar red pimento strips
1 small can or jar black olives
1 small can or jar green olives
1 jar marinated artichokes
1 can frozen lemonade concentrate
1 4-oz. can deviled ham
1 can sardines
1 loaf sourdough bread
1 bottle light, dry red wine, claret or equivalent, French or Californian
1 bottle or ½ bottle Puerto Rican rum, light

MENU

STRAWBERRY DAIQUIRI

HORS D'OEUVRES PLATTER

BASQUE TORTILLA DIABLO

LIGHT DRY RED WINE

**SLICED ORANGES WITH STRAWBERRIES
BLACK COFFEE**

1 PRELIMINARIES

Arrange appetizer platter, putting the various ingredients in groups so that they contrast in color. Strips of pimento can be laid across the asparagus, and a little chopped parsley sprinkled over the sardines. Cover with plastic wrap, and chill in the refrigerator.

Peel the oranges, taking off all the white pith as well as the outside peels. Slice in rings, and arrange around the edge of a large plate. Wash the strawberries and drain them. Put a large, perfect strawberry on each orange slice, and pile the rest of them in the middle, saving 6 or 8 for the strawberry daiquiris. Sprinkle with sugar, cover with plastic wrap, and refrigerate.

2 PREPARING THE MAIN DISH

INGREDIENTS:

1 medium onion, diced
1 medium-size green pepper, diced
1 tbsp. oil
1 4-oz. can deviled ham
1 medium tomato, diced
2 tbsp. butter

8 eggs, lightly beaten with a dash of Tabasco
$\frac{1}{2}$ tsp. salt
$\frac{1}{4}$ tsp. pepper
1 tomato, quartered

METHOD:

Sauté diced onion and green pepper in oil until tender. Add deviled ham and diced tomato. Keep warm over low heat.

Melt butter in a large heavy skillet; add eggs mixed with salt and pepper, and cook over moderate heat. As omelet begins to set, carefully lift edges with a spatula and let uncooked portion run under.

When omelet is set but top is still soft, pour deviled ham mixture over top, and spread evenly. Cook 1 minute more. Cut omelet into wedges, and garnish each with a tomato quarter.

The best plan is to serve the drinks and the appetizer platter *before* you cook the omelet. You may have to keep your guests waiting for a few minutes while you complete the omelet, but it will be less likely to get tough than if you prepare it before they sit down at the table.

3 SERVING THE BRUNCH

Prepare strawberry daiquiris in the blender or shaker. Put in 1 c. crushed or flaked ice, 4 jiggers rum, 3 tbsp. frozen lemonade concentrate, and the 6–8 strawberries. Blend or shake until smooth and frothy, and pour into chilled glasses.

Bring out the appetizer platter along with the sourdough bread (heated, wrapped in foil for 10 minutes until crisp in the oven), and sweet butter.

Offer a second round of drinks, then disappear into the kitchen to finish the tortilla diablo. Serve on warmed plates with tomato wedges as garnish. Pour the wine.

Dessert: orange-strawberry platter sprinkled with a little Cognac or liqueur if available.

Finish with strong black coffee.

BRUNCH NUMBER 6
SERVES SIX

MENU

SALTY DOG

HOT STRAINED BORSCHT

GYPSY'S CHEF'S SALAD
HARD ROLLS

SLIGHTLY SPARKLING ROSÉ

LIME SHERBET
ESPRESSO

Check your supply shelf for the following; if missing any item, add to marketing list:

Egg (1)
Butter
Oil ($\frac{1}{2}$ c.)
Red wine vinegar
Worcestershire sauce
Dry mustard
Lemons (2)
Garlic
Salt, pepper
Espresso coffee

MARKETING LIST

$\frac{1}{4}$ lb.-slice boiled or
    baked ham
$\frac{1}{4}$ lb. cooked turkey roll
    or cooked
    chicken
$\frac{1}{4}$ lb.-piece of salami   from
$\frac{1}{4}$ lb.-slice of cooked   delicatessen
    smoked tongue
    (if not available,
    buy a glass jar of
    beef or calf
    tongue)
1 jar grated Parmesan cheese
1 package natural Swiss cheese
    (4–6 oz.)
1 small package blue cheese
1 large or 2 small heads romaine
1 bunch green onions
2 large tomatoes
1 can grapefruit juice
1 quart jar borscht
1 2-oz. can flat anchovy fillets
1–2 packages bake-and-serve hard
    rolls (allow $1\frac{1}{2}$ rolls per person)
1 quart lime sherbet
2 bottles sparkling rosé, such as
    Mateus or Lancers
1 bottle vodka

1 PREPARING THE MAIN DISH

INGREDIENTS:

Salad:

$\frac{1}{2}$ c. each turkey or chicken, ham, tongue, salami, and Swiss cheese, cut in strips
1 head romaine lettuce
2 green onions
2 tomatoes

Dressing:

1 egg
1 tbsp. blue cheese

1 clove garlic, crushed
$\frac{1}{2}$ tsp. dry mustard
Salt, pepper
$\frac{1}{2}$ c. oil
Dash of Worcestershire sauce
$\frac{1}{2}$ lemon
1 tbsp. red wine vinegar
$\frac{1}{2}$ c. shredded Parmesan cheese
1 2-oz. can anchovy fillets

METHOD:

Chill rosé wine in refrigerator.

Wash, drain, and dry the romaine. Tear into bite-size pieces, and put in a large salad bowl. Add the meats and cheese (strips should be $\frac{1}{4}$–$\frac{1}{2}$-inch wide, no bigger). Chop 2 green onions, quarter the tomatoes, and add these to the salad bowl. Refrigerate.

Prepare the dressing as follows: Cook the egg 1 minute in simmering water.

Mash the blue cheese with a fork; put in a mixing bowl. Add crushed garlic clove, dry mustard, salt, and pepper, and stir well. Gradually add oil, stirring well, then add Worcestershire sauce and cooked egg; stir again to blend thoroughly. Chill until serving time. Drain anchovy fillets.

Strain borscht and heat. Bake the hard rolls according to package directions.

2 SERVING THE BRUNCH

Make salty dogs in tall narrow glasses: Rub the edge of each glass with cut lemon, then dip each into a saucer of coarse salt so that the edge is coated. Pour into each glass 1 jigger of vodka and 3 or 4 jiggers of grapefruit juice (proportions may be varied according to taste).

Ladle hot borscht into cups.

Just before serving the salad, squeeze over it the juice of $\frac{1}{2}$ lemon, and sprinkle with 1 tbsp. vinegar. Stir to mix dressing. Sprinkle with Parmesan cheese, and arrange anchovy strips across top of salad. Bring to the table, and toss again before serving. Arrange hot rolls and butter on a tray. Pour the rosé wine.

Dessert: lime sherbet, followed by small cups of espresso with lemon twist.

BRUNCH NUMBER 7
SERVES TWO

SUPPLY CHECKLIST
Check your supply shelf for the following; if missing any item, add to marketing list:

Butter
Bread crumbs
Flour
Coffee
Salt, pepper
Tabasco
Salad dressing
Vodka

MARKETING LIST
8 large raw oysters
½ lb. bacon
½ dozen eggs
1 bunch parsley
1 lb. tomatoes
1 loaf oatmeal bread
1 can frozen orange juice
Apple strudel, frozen or from bakery

MENU

SCREWDRIVER

HANGTOWN FRY
TOMATO SALAD
TOASTED OATMEAL BREAD

COFFEE

APPLE STRUDEL

1 PRELIMINARIES

Wash, dry, and slice tomatoes. Arrange in shallow bowl. Sprinkle with 1 tbsp. chopped parsley, and pour over them 2–3 tbsp. salad dressing. Chill.

Mix the orange juice.

Heat frozen strudel according to directions. If not frozen, crisp it for 5 minutes in a 400° oven just before serving time.

2 PREPARING THE MAIN DISH

INGREDIENTS:

8 raw oysters	4 slices bacon, cut in half and cooked
Flour	5 large eggs
1 beaten egg	Salt, pepper
½ c. bread crumbs	Tabasco
½ stick butter	

METHOD:

Dip oysters in flour, then in beaten egg, then in bread crumbs. Melt butter in skillet, and sauté oysters 1 minute on each side. Arrange cooked bacon slices in pan with oysters. Beat 5 eggs with salt, pepper, and a dash of Tabasco. Pour mixture over oysters and bacon, and cook slowly until eggs are set. Lift sides of omelet gently to allow uncooked eggs to run underneath. Put under broiler to brown top slightly if desired. Do not overcook.

Brew coffee while omelet is cooking.

Wrap oatmeal bread in foil, and heat in 400° oven for 10 minutes.

3 SERVING THE BRUNCH

For screwdrivers, shake with ice 2 jiggers vodka and 6 jiggers orange juice. Strain into two chilled glasses.

Serve hangtown fry on warmed plates, with buttered oatmeal toast. Bring out the tomato salad, and pour hot coffee.

Dessert: apple strudel; refill the coffee cups.

BRUNCH NUMBER 8
SERVES FOUR

SUPPLY CHECKLIST
Check your supply shelf for the following; if missing any item, add to marketing list:
Milk
Butter
Flour
Bread crumbs
Coffee
Dry mustard
Salt, pepper
Lemon

MARKETING LIST
1 lb. sausage meat or link sausage
1 dozen eggs, medium or small size
2 small cantaloupes
1 package hashed brown potato mix
4 large dill pickles
1 package oatcakes or 1 loaf oatmeal
    bread
2 small or 1 large can homogenized
    shortening (Crisco, Spry, etc.)
1 pint vanilla ice cream
Scotch whiskey (fifth or pint)
Stone's or Crabbie's ginger wine
Dry vermouth

MENU

WHISKEY MAC

SCOTCH EGGS
HASHED BROWN POTATOES, DILL PICKLES
OATCAKES

COFFEE

CANTALOUPE

1 PREPARING THE MAIN DISH

All but the final frying can be done the day before.

INGREDIENTS:

6 eggs	1 tsp. dry mustard
1 lb. sausage meat	1½ c. milk
Bread crumbs	Salt, pepper
2 eggs, beaten	Homogenized shortening or oil for frying
2 tbsp. flour	(should be 4 or more inches deep
2 tbsp. butter	in a large heavy pan)

METHOD:

Hard-boil 6 eggs by putting in cold salted water, bringing to a boil, and simmering for 10 minutes. Cool and shell. Take sausage meat out of its casing, divide into 6 portions, and pat them out on a floured board so that they are 4–5 inches long by 3 inches wide. Wrap each piece of sausage meat carefully around a hard-boiled egg, pinching the edges together so there are no gaps. Dip in the beaten eggs, then roll in bread crumbs so they are completely coated. If there are any bald spots, dip and coat a second time. Set aside, overnight if possible, until 15 minutes before serving time. Make the mustard sauce as follows: melt 2 tbsp. butter in a saucepan, stir in 2 tbsp. flour and 1 tsp. dry mustard. Stir in gradually 1½ c. milk, and heat to boiling point, stirring with a whisk until it is smooth and thickened. Season with salt and pepper, and keep warm until serving time.

Prepare hashed brown potatoes according to package directions. While they are cooking, melt and heat frying fat or oil in a heavy saucepan. The correct temperature for frying the Scotch eggs is 365°. If you have a fat thermometer, this is easy to check, but if you don't have one, test the temperature by dropping in a small cube of stale white bread. At 365° the bread will drop to the bottom, bob up again, and change color to golden brown in 1 minute by the clock. This is the right temperature for frying your Scotch eggs. If the fat is too cool, fried foods get soggy and greasy; if it's too hot (smoking), foods burn on the outside before they are cooked through.

Lower the Scotch eggs gently into the hot fat, or use a frying basket, and allow them to cook 5 or 6 minutes until well browned. Lift out, and drain on folded paper towels. Keep warm until serving time.

Brew coffee or make instant coffee in an attractive serving pot.

2 SERVING THE BRUNCH

Make whiskey Macs as follows: Put ice cubes in a cocktail shaker, add 4 jiggers Scotch whiskey, 2 jiggers Stone's or Crabbie's ginger wine, and 2 jiggers dry vermouth. Shake well, and strain over ice cubes into old-fashioned glasses, adding a twist of lemon peel. If you can't find ginger wine, substitute 1 jigger sweet vermouth (for a Rob Roy).

To serve the Scotch eggs, cut each egg in half across, and arrange 3 halves on each plate with the mustard sauce spooned over. Add a scoop of hashed brown potatoes and a dill pickle sliced like a fan (not all the way down to the stem end) as a garnish. Offer oatcake or toasted oatmeal bread. Pour hot coffee.

Dessert: small cantaloupe halves with the centers hollowed out and filled with a scoop of vanilla ice cream.

BRUNCH NUMBER 9
SERVES FOUR

SUPPLY CHECKLIST
Check your supply shelf for the following; if missing any item, add to marketing list:

Butter
Lemons (2)
Curry powder
Salt, pepper
Worcestershire sauce
Rose's lime juice (sweetened)
Gin
Coffee

MARKETING LIST
$\frac{3}{4}$–1 lb. finnan haddie or smoked cod fillet
$\frac{1}{2}$ dozen eggs
$\frac{1}{2}$ lb. bacon
1 bunch parsley
1 bunch green onions
1 cucumber
1 can mangoes
1 jar chutney
1 package rice (white, long grain)
1 package heat-and-serve butterflake rolls

MENU

GIMLET

KEDGEREE
BUTTERFLAKE ROLLS

COFFEE

CHILLED MANGO SLICES

1 PREPARING THE MAIN DISH

The kedgeree may be cooked the day before; heat at serving time.

INGREDIENTS:

¾–1 lb. finnan haddie or smoked cod fillet
4 eggs
1½ c. raw rice
4 tbsp. butter
2 tbsp. chopped parsley

1 tbsp., or to taste, curry powder
1 tbsp. Worcestershire sauce
Salt, pepper
2 tbsp. lemon juice

METHOD:

Cook finnan haddie 7–10 minutes in simmering water. Drain and cool. Cook rice in boiling salted water according to package directions. Hard-boil eggs and cool; shell, and chop coarsely, leaving aside one yolk.

Take bones, skin, and any tough or dark edges off finnan haddie, and flake with a fork or a silver knife. Melt butter in a heavy saucepan, and add flaked fish and chopped hard-boiled egg. Add drained rice and parsley; season with curry powder, Worcestershire sauce, salt, pepper, and lemon juice. Stir and simmer for a few minutes to blend flavors, adding more butter if the mixture seems dry. Reheat over low flame just before serving time.

Cook bacon strips (2 or 3 for each guest) until crisp; drain and keep warm. Wash, trim, and chop green onions, and put in a small bowl or side dish. Peel and slice cucumber; put in a bowl, and sprinkle with salt and freshly grated pepper. Fill a third bowl with chutney, and arrange the three bowls on a small tray.

Heat butterflake rolls according to package directions, and brew a pot of good, strong coffee.

2 SERVING THE BRUNCH

At serving time, mix gimlets, using 6 jiggers gin to 1½ jiggers Rose's lime juice. Shake with ice, strain into cold glasses, and add a splash of soda if desired.

Put the piping hot kedgeree in a mound on a serving platter. Push the reserved egg yolk through a sieve or strainer over the top, and garnish with a ring of bacon strips and lemon sections. Accompany kedgeree by hot rolls, plenty of coffee, and the tray of relishes.

Dessert: chilled mango slices or pulp in small bowls, and additional rounds of hot coffee.

BRUNCH NUMBER 10
SERVES TWO

SUPPLY CHECKLIST
Check your supply shelf for the following; if missing any item, add to marketing list:

Flour
Milk (1 quart)
Eggs (2)
Oil
Butter
Salt, pepper
Lump sugar
Angostura bitters
Brandy (Cognac or California)

MARKETING LIST
$\frac{1}{2}$ lb. cooked turkey roll or 1 can
    boneless chicken
1 package frozen broccoli or 1 bunch
    fresh broccoli
1 package heat-and-serve sesame
    rolls
1 jar grated Parmesan cheese
1 bottle champagne

MENU

RAJAH'S PEG

CRÊPES DE VOLAILLE GRATINÉES
BUTTERED BROCCOLI
SESAME-SEED ROLLS

CHAMPAGNE

DUTCH CHOCOLATE ICE CREAM

1 PREPARING THE MAIN DISH

The crêpes can be prepared the day before and finished just before serving time.

INGREDIENTS:

Pancakes:	Filling and Sauce:
$\frac{1}{2}$ c. flour	3 tbsp. butter
$\frac{1}{2}$ tsp. salt	3 tbsp. flour
2 eggs	$1\frac{1}{2}$–2 c. milk
$\frac{1}{2}$ c. milk	Salt, pepper
$\frac{1}{4}$ c. water	1 cup chicken or turkey, cooked and cubed
2 tbsp. oil or melted butter	Grated Parmesan cheese

METHOD:

Mix the pancake batter first: Sift flour and salt together into a bowl. Break in the eggs, one at a time, and after each addition, stir and mix in the flour. The mixture will be stiff and somewhat lumpy. Gradually add milk, blending with an electric or a rotary beater until smooth. When all the milk is in, add oil or melted butter and water. Beat for another few minutes; then set aside for about 1 hour.

Make sauce: Melt butter in a saucepan, stir in flour until smooth. Off the flame, stir in milk, a little at a time. Add salt and pepper. Put back on low flame, and bring to the boil, stirring and beating with a small whisk so that it does not get lumpy. Stir until thickened, and simmer for a few minutes. Put turkey or chicken cubes into a small pan, add about half the sauce, and cook gently until chicken is heated and blended with sauce. Add more seasoning (salt, pepper, Worcestershire sauce) if necessary.

Beat the pancake batter again for several minutes. Lightly grease a crêpe pan, or small skillet with sloping sides, and heat over a moderately low flame until grease just begins to turn golden brown (a Teflon pan works fine, but it should not be more than about 6 inches across the bottom). Then quickly pour in $1\frac{1}{2}$–2 tbsp. of the batter, and swirl it around to cover the bottom of the pan with a very thin layer. It will begin to brown underneath almost immediately. With a spatula or knife or even with your fingers, pick up the edge of the pancake and look at it; if it's browned, turn it over. The second side will cook even faster. You can guess at the quantity to pour into the pan, but it's easiest to use a very small ladle or a $\frac{1}{4}$-cup measure only *half* full, so that all the cakes will be the same thickness. As each pancake is cooked, lay it on a clean dish towel, and start on another. This amount of batter will make 9 or 10 6-inch pancakes, so if you break or scorch a few, it is not a disaster; you will still have enough.

Using 3 or 4 pancakes for each serving, divide the chicken mixture between them, spreading it toward one side in a finger-shaped roll. Then roll each pancake so that it encloses the filling, and place seam side down in a baking dish. If prepared ahead of time, cover with plastic wrap and refrigerate. Pour 2 tbsp. of milk or cream over the top of the remaining sauce, and refrigerate.

Chill the champagne overnight.

2 FINAL ASSEMBLY

Half an hour before serving, turn oven to 400°.

Cook broccoli according to directions. Drain and keep warm. Heat sesame rolls according to package directions.

Take chicken pancakes and sauce out of refrigerator. Heat and stir the sauce over a low flame, and add a little more milk or cream if necessary to make it a pouring consistency. Pour the sauce over the pancakes, and sprinkle with grated cheese. Put in oven until hot and bubbly, 15–20 minutes. (Crêpes can be baked in individual oval gratin dishes if you have them.) If not sufficiently brown, put the pancakes under the broiler briefly.

3 SERVING THE BRUNCH

Mix the rajah's peg by putting a lump of sugar in each glass. (Tall narrow flute glasses or small Pilsner glasses are the best shape.) Splash a few drops of Angostura bitters on each sugar cube, then add 1 jigger of brandy to each, and fill with champagne. You don't need to use expensive imported champagne for this; any dry champagne from California or New York State will make an excellent peg.

Bring out the crêpes de volaille accompanied by buttered broccoli and hot rolls. Pour the rest of the champagne into the same glasses throughout the meal.

Dessert: dutch chocolate ice cream with 1 tsp. crème de menthe on top.

BRUNCH NUMBER 11

SERVES TWO

SUPPLY CHECKLIST

Check your supply shelf for the following; if missing any item, add to marketing list:

Butter
Dijon-style mustard
Mayonnaise
Salt, pepper
Vodka
Sugar
Worcestershire sauce
Tabasco

MARKETING LIST

$\frac{1}{2}$ lb. thickly sliced bacon
$\frac{1}{2}$ dozen eggs
2 lemons
1 small cauliflower
1 bunch parsley
1 lb. firm potatoes, preferably new
     potatoes
1 package mixed dried fruit
1 package or loaf pumpernickel bread
$\frac{1}{2}$ pint heavy cream
1 can tomato juice
2–3 bottles light, dry lager beer

MENU

BLOODY MARY

FARMER'S BREAKFAST
COLD CAULIFLOWER SPRIGS
PUMPERNICKEL AND BUTTER

LAGER BEER

MIXED DRIED FRUIT COMPOTE

1 PRELIMINARIES

Chill beer in refrigerator.

Prepare fruit compote: Soak dried fruit overnight in enough water to cover. Make a syrup with 1 c. sugar to 2 c. water; bring to boil slowly, and simmer for 10 minutes. Put soaked, drained fruit in an ovenproof casserole with a lid. Pour syrup over, and add the thin yellow peel of 1 lemon. Put in a slow oven (250°), and cook until fruit is very tender but not mushy, about 40–60 minutes. Remove **lemon peel,** and chill fruit in refrigerator.

Divide cauliflower into sprigs 1–1½ inches across, and trim off stalk. Cook until just tender but still a little crisp, in boiling salted water. Drain and arrange in a platter or shallow bowl, and chill. Mix 1 tbsp. Dijon-style mustard with 3 tbsp. mayonnaise; add 1 tbsp. cream and 1 tsp. lemon juice. Beat together and chill.

2 PREPARING THE MAIN DISH

INGREDIENTS:

4 medium-size potatoes	**$\frac{1}{4}$ tsp. salt**
6 slices thickly cut bacon	**$\frac{1}{4}$ tsp. pepper**
4 eggs	**Chopped parsley for garnish**

METHOD:

Scrub potatoes, and boil them in their skins until just tender, about 15–20 minutes. Cool, peel, and chill. (This would be good to do ahead of time, so that potatoes are cold and firm.)

Dice bacon strips, and cook slowly until crisp and brown. Lift out with a slotted spoon or a fork, leaving the fat in the pan. Cut cold potatoes into ½-inch cubes, and cook them in the hot bacon fat until brown. Drain off fat, and add potato to bacon cubes. Beat 2 eggs slightly, and put in a cup; then beat the other 2, and put into a second cup. Divide the salt and pepper between them.

Lightly butter a small skillet, not larger than 6–7 inches across the bottom (a Teflon pan gives good results). Put in it half the bacon-potato mixture in an even layer. Heat over a moderate flame for about 1 minute, then pour in 2 of the beaten eggs. Allow to cook gently, while lifting at the sides to allow the uncooked eggs to run underneath. Cook until almost set but still a little creamy on top, then fold in half with a spatula and turn out onto a hot platter. Wipe the pan with a paper towel if there are any bits stuck to it, grease lightly again, and repeat the process for the second omelet. Put the platter containing the two omelets over a pan of hot but not boiling water, on the lowest possible flame, and cover with a lid to keep warm until serving.

3 SERVING THE BRUNCH

Mix bloody Marys: Shake with ice 2 jiggers vodka, 4 jiggers tomato juice, the juice of 1 lemon, and a dash each of Worcestershire sauce and Tabasco. Strain into two glasses, on the rocks or straight up, and grind a little black pepper onto the top.

Pour mustard-mayonnaise dressing over the cauliflower sprigs, and sprinkle with paprika.

For the main course, sprinkle chopped parsley on farmer's breakfast omelets. Serve the cauliflower salad, pumpernickel, and butter. Pour ice-cold beer.

Dessert: fruit compote, with heavy cream to pour over it; have a pot of coffee ready and hot.

BRUNCH NUMBER 12
SERVES FOUR

SUPPLY CHECKLIST
Check your supply shelf for the following; if missing any item, add to marketing list:
Butter
Milk
Flour
Grated cheese, Parmesan or Swiss
Salt, peppercorns
Tabasco
Sherry (4 tbsp.)
Espresso

MARKETING LIST
1 slice halibut or swordfish (8–12 oz. without bone)
1 dozen medium shrimps
½ dozen large scallops or 1 dozen small ones
1 can frozen orange juice
2 packages frozen green peas
1 small jar red pimento
1–2 packages heat-and-serve croissants (allow 2 for each person)
1 package frozen brownies or 1 brownie mix
1 pint vanilla ice cream
½ bottle champagne (California or New York)
2 bottles Alsatian white wine such as Sylvaner or Riesling

MENU

ORANGE JUICE AND CHAMPAGNE

COQUILLES DE FRUITS DE MER
GREEN PEAS
CROISSANTS

ALSATIAN WINE

BROWNIE SQUARES

1 PREPARING THE MAIN DISH

The coquilles can be prepared the day before and finished at serving time.

INGREDIENTS:

1 slice halibut or swordfish
$\frac{1}{2}$ dozen large scallops or 1 dozen small
1 dozen medium shrimps
6 tbsp. butter, plus extra to dot on coquilles
4 tbsp. flour
$\frac{3}{4}$–1 c. milk
Salt, peppercorns
4 tbsp. grated cheese
4 tbsp. sherry
Tabasco

METHOD:

Cook halibut or swordfish in enough lightly salted boiling water to cover it, over low heat, 7–10 minutes. Lift out of water, and set to cool. In the same cooking water, simmer the scallops 4–5 minutes. Drain and cool, saving the cooking liquid. Cook shrimps in fresh, well-salted water for 5 minutes, adding 2 or 3 peppercorns to the water. Drain and cool, discarding the water. Shell the shrimps, and remove the dark veins from the backs; if large, cut in half. If using large scallops, divide into pieces no more than $\frac{3}{4}$ to 1 inch across. Remove all skin and bone from the slice of fish, and cut into neat cubes $\frac{3}{4}$ to 1 inch across.

Melt 4 tbsp. butter in saucepan, and stir in flour, smoothing out any lumps. Away from the flame, add 1 c. of the reserved cooking liquid from the fish, a little at a time, stirring it in thoroughly; add $\frac{3}{4}$ c. of milk, and put back on the fire. Stir and beat with a whisk until it comes to the boil and thickens. Add the sherry and a dash of Tabasco, and simmer for 5 minutes to blend. Carefully add the fish, the shrimps, and the scallops to the sauce and heat gently. Season with a little pepper and salt if necessary (keep in mind that there was salt in the cooking liquid). If the sauce is very thick, add 1 or 2 tsps. more milk. Whether this is necessary or not depends on how moist the fish, shrimps, and scallops are when added to the sauce. Divide the mixture among four individual baking dishes or casseroles, which may be pottery, glass, or copper, or even large scallop shells.

If made ahead of time, cover with plastic wrap and refrigerate until 1 hour before serving time.

Chill wine and champagne overnight if possible.

2 FINAL ASSEMBLY

On the day of the party, mix the frozen orange juice, and chill in refrigerator. Remove casseroles from refrigerator, and let stand till almost at room temperature. Heat oven to 375°. Sprinkle coquilles with Parmesan cheese and dot with butter. Bake for 20 minutes, until hot and bubbly; then raise heat, and put under the broiler for 5–10 minutes, until top is glazed and golden brown. Turn heat down low, and open oven door to cool so that coquilles just keep warm.

While coquilles are baking, cook the green peas, drain, and add 2 tbsp. butter and 2 tbsp. diced pimento.

Heat croissants as package says.

3 SERVING THE BRUNCH

Using wineglasses, tall narrow glasses, or small goblets, pour half full of orange juice, fill with chilled champagne. Mix gently and serve promptly.

For the main course, bring out the coquilles de fruits de mer with pimento-garnished green peas. Put hot croissants in a basket. Pour the wine.

Dessert: brownie squares or slices, each topped with a small scoop of ice cream.

Finish with espresso.

CHAPTER 6

SEDUCTIVE SWEETS

The following recipes are given as *variations* for the desserts suggested in the dinner menus. As they are slightly more elaborate, you can also use them as the *pièce de résistance* for a dessert *party* . . . a good solution when preparation time is limited, or if you want to invite more people than you can manage for dinner. Sometimes it's fun (and easy!) if one hostess entertains guests for the first half of the meal, then escorts everyone to somebody else's house for dessert and coffee. This plan divides the work between two hostesses, either of whom would be overloaded if she had to cope with the whole meal.

Whether you serve guests at the dinner table or grouped informally in the living room, the dessert party is an occasion for a really glamorous presentation. Have plenty of flowers and candles, and use your prettiest linen and silver. Everything can be set up (and cooked!) ahead of time, and only a minimum of service is needed when guests arrive.

Coffee, tea, wine, or punch are all good drink possibilities at a dessert party; cocktails don't belong here, though liqueurs and brandy may be offered with coffee after the dessert.

Chapter 7 covers drinks in greater detail, and some of those beverages are appropriate for serving with dessert. If you want to serve wine, choose white rather than red, and don't pick one that is too dry; the sweetness of the dessert makes a dry wine taste thin and sharp. A French Sauterne is appropriate, or some of the white wines of the Burgundy district, such as Chablis, Montrachet, Pouilly-Fuissé; so are some of the less dry wines of the Moselle Valley or the Rhine, such as Bernkasteler, Niersteiner, or Schloss Johannisberger. Perhaps the most delicious is a sparkling white wine, such as Vouvray (French), Asti Spumanti (Italian), or, of course, champagne, whether French, Californian, or New York State. Actually there are versions of champagne from practically every wine-producing country, and some are delicious, though less well known than the French prototype. You may find sparkling white wines, similar to champagne, from Germany, Hungary, Yugoslavia, Turkey, Australia, South Africa. If you want to be on the safe side, sample one bottle a few days before the party. If you decide it's not quite super enough as is, make a champagne punch (delicious!), or serve the rajah's peg, a marvelous drink described under Brunch Menu Number 10.

One word of caution: It's not wise to serve a dessert involving gobs of whipped cream at a very crowded party, where some of the guests may be standing up and possibly even bumping into each other. Spilled whipped cream can be a first-class mess on clothes, rugs, and cushions. Safer to serve cookies or nongooey desserts, so that a spill isn't a disaster.

1 BLUEBERRY RUM TARTS
SERVES SIX

2 c. blueberries, fresh, canned, or thawed frozen
$2\frac{1}{2}$ tbsp. cornstarch
1 c. water
$\frac{1}{2}$ c. sugar
$\frac{1}{4}$ tsp. salt
$\frac{1}{8}$ tsp. nutmeg
$\frac{1}{4}$ c. rum
1 tbsp. lemon juice
6 tart shells, from bakery or frozen
$\frac{1}{2}$ pt. heavy cream, to whip for topping

Wash berries, drain thoroughly. Mix cornstarch smoothly with water; add sugar, salt, and nutmeg, and cook over medium heat for 5 minutes until mixture is thick and transparent. Stir in rum, lemon juice, and berries. Pour into tart shells, and refrigerate. You can whip the cream an hour or two ahead and refrigerate it; chill the wire whisk and bowl, and the cream will whip quickly. *Just* before serving, decorate the chilled tarts with whipped cream topping.

2 STRAWBERRY VALENTINE SOUFFLE
SERVES SIX

1 envelope plain, unflavored gelatin
$\frac{1}{4}$ c. cold water
1 3-oz. package cream cheese, at room temperature
$\frac{1}{4}$ c. sugar
1 c. boiling water
1 tsp. lemon juice
$\frac{3}{4}$ c. sliced frozen strawberries, mashed
$\frac{1}{2}$ pint heavy cream, to whip
1 package candy hearts

Build up the rim of a soufflé dish by wrapping a folded strip of waxed paper or aluminum foil around the outside of the dish; anchor it in place with string or a rubber band. It should rise 2 inches higher than the top of the dish, like a collar. Brush the inside of the dish and the collar lightly with oil.

Sprinkle gelatin onto $\frac{1}{4}$ c. water, and set aside. Beat cream cheese with fork, and blend in sugar.

Dissolve softened gelatin in 1 c. boiling water, and add to cream cheese mixture, along with lemon juice. Cool in refrigerator until it begins to solidify. Meanwhile, whip $\frac{3}{4}$ c. of cream, using chilled bowl and whisk. When the gelatin mixture is about the consistency of raw egg whites, fold in mashed berries and about $\frac{2}{3}$ of the whipped cream, making *very* gentle down-and-sideways strokes with a rubber spatula. Turn carefully into soufflé dish, and chill until firm. Remove paper collar from the dish (slowly, so as not to disturb the mixture, which may cling to it). Decorate top of soufflé with swirls of remaining whipped cream and a design of candy hearts. Keep very cold until serving time.

3 FRENCH CHOCOLATE MOUSSE
SERVES FOUR TO SIX

1 package semisweet chocolate (or 1 6-oz. package chocolate chips)
2 tbsp. water

4 eggs, separated
$\frac{1}{4}$ tsp. salt
1 tsp. vanilla

Break chocolate into pieces (or use chips), and put in the top of a double boiler or in a small bowl that will fit on top of a saucepan. Add the water and the salt. Put 2–3 inches boiling water in the bottom of the double boiler or in the pan you are using under a bowl. Put over low heat, so that the chocolate melts. Stir occasionally, until melted and smooth. Beat egg yolks until thick and creamy; add them with the vanilla to the melted chocolate. Beat the egg whites until very stiff, in a copper bowl if you have one. (If you use the same beater that you used for the egg yolks, it must be washed, rinsed, and dried *thoroughly* be-fore beating the egg whites. Another help is to chill the beater and bowl.)

When the egg whites hold a firm peak, fold them carefully into the chocolate mixture, cutting down and flipping the mixture lightly over with a rubber spatula until it is well blended. Pour into small bowls or soufflé dishes, and chill until firm. Decorate the top with a few chopped walnuts or almonds. The recipe makes enough to serve four—this is a deliciously rich dessert, and you need only small portions. If you wish, put a dollop of whipped cream on top.

4 APPLE CAKE
SERVES SIX

A very good simple dessert.

$\frac{1}{2}$ c. flour
$\frac{3}{4}$ c. sugar
$\frac{1}{4}$ tsp. salt
1 tsp. baking powder

1 c. diced apples
$\frac{1}{2}$ c. chopped walnuts or pecans
1 tsp. vanilla
1 egg, beaten

Sift flour, sugar, salt, and baking powder into a bowl. Add apples, nuts, vanilla, and egg, and mix thoroughly. Put into a greased, shallow baking dish, and bake in moderate (350°) oven until brown and crisp, about 30 minutes. Serve warm, topped with whipped cream or vanilla ice cream.

5 GINGERBREAD IMPERIAL
SERVES SIX TO EIGHT

1 package gingerbread mix
1 package mincemeat mix
¼ c. sherry

¼ c. coarsely chopped walnuts
Powdered or frosting sugar

Mix gingerbread according to package directions, but bake in 2 small pans of the same shape and size—7-inch square pans or 8-inch pie tins are good. They will cook in about 10 minutes less time than in a large tin. Test to be sure they are cooked through by inserting a toothpick; when it comes out dry, cake is done. Remove from oven, and cool on a rack.

Reconstitute mincemeat according to package directions, but use only half the quantity of water specified. When the mincemeat is blended and hot, add sherry and coarsely chopped walnuts. Cool mixture until lukewarm.

Turn one portion of gingerbread upside down, and spread the surface thickly with the mincemeat mixture. Put the other portion, face up, on top of it, and lightly press down to make it stick to the mincemeat filling. Put a lacy paper doily on top of the upper layer, and sift powdered or frosting sugar evenly all over it. Lift doily very carefully from both sides, and you will have a decorative sugar design on the cake. The gingerbread should be served warm or at room temperature.

If desired, serve with whipped cream or a sauce of 1 3-oz. package of cream cheese beaten with 2 tbsp. sugar and enough milk or light cream to make it a thick, pouring consistency. Keep the sauce cool until serving time.

6 POUND CAKE EN SURPRISE
SERVES SIX

1 pound cake, baked according to package directions in a small loaf tin, or from bakery

1 pint coffee ice cream (square is best)
½ pint whipping cream
Walnuts or grated chocolate for garnish

Prepare at least one day ahead.

Trim the outside browned surfaces off the pound cake, and cut carefully into nine even slices. Cut ice cream into eight even slices—use a knife dipped into hot water for easier cutting. Alternate a slice of cake and a slice of ice cream, beginning and ending with cake, in a large loaf tin, or wrap in foil and put back into the freezer to freeze firm. If you use the freez-ing compartment of the refrigerator, turn the control to the coldest temperature.

Shortly before serving time, whip the cream using a chilled whisk and bowl. Take the ice cream cake out of the tin or its foil wrapping, and frost it quickly with the whipped cream. Garnish with walnuts or grated chocolate. Present the cake to your guests, then cut and serve on dessert plates at the table.

7 MERINGUES

Homemade meringues are really very easy, and so much more delicious than the store-bought variety. You can make them several days ahead, as they keep fresh for quite a long time. The quan-tities given are enough to serve four; if you need only two servings, either halve the recipe or make the full quantity and store the extra meringues in a tin for future use (alone or in other recipes).

BASIC MERINGUE RECIPE
(makes 8–10 meringues)

4 egg whites	**$\frac{1}{2}$ tsp. vanilla**
$\frac{1}{4}$ tsp. salt	**1 tsp. vinegar**
1 c. sugar	**Brown wrapping paper**

Preheat oven to 250°

Separate 4 eggs carefully, and put whites into a very large chilled bowl. There must be no flecks of yolk *at all* in the whites. Add salt to egg whites, beat with electric beater at high speed or a large chilled whisk until stiff enough to stand up in peaks. At low speed, gradually beat in sifted sugar, 2–3 tbsp. at a time. Continue until all sugar is added, adding vanilla and vinegar during this beating process. The mixture will be very thick, quite glossy and shining.

Line a large, flat baking sheet with brown wrapping paper. Mark circles on the paper with the bottom of a glass to spoon the dough into, so all the meringues will be the same size and shape. Scoop the mixture out of the bowl with a table-spoon, then scrape it out of the tablespoon and onto the baking sheet with a teaspoon. The mounds of dough should be about the size and shape of a half orange. The surface can be smoothed, if necessary, with a knife dipped in hot water.

Bake at 250° for 1 hour. Check to see if insides are dry and not sticky by inserting the point of a smaller knife in the thickest part, and if necessary, allow an extra 10–15 minutes. When fully cooked to a pale, creamy color, turn off the heat, open the oven door, and allow them to finish drying for about another ½ hour, then cool.

THREE WAYS TO SERVE MERINGUES:
Meringues Glacées

Sandwich two meringues with a scoop of ice cream between them.

Pluperfect Parfait (serves four)

3–4 meringues (left over from basic recipe, or make half batch)
1 pint vanilla ice cream
1 package frozen raspberries or other frozen or fresh fruit
½ c. whipping cream

Use parfait glasses or goblets; they should be deep and fairly narrow. Break meringues up into small pieces, no more than 1 inch across. Partly thaw frozen fruit. Whip the cream, using a chilled bowl and whisk.

Fill the glasses with alternating layers of meringue, ice cream, and fruit. See that each glass contains an equal amount of all three ingredients. Top with dollops of whipped cream, and set out long-handled spoons to eat with.

Foam Pie

Heat oven to 250°.

Prepare basic meringue mixture. Line a baking sheet with heavy brown paper, and trace a large circle on it. Use a service plate or a large dinner plate if you are serving 8–10 people; for 4–6 servings, trace around a 9-inch pie tin.

Spread an even layer of meringue dough over the whole circle, about ¾ inch thick. It may be smoothed a little with a knife or spatula, but need not be absolutely flat. Around the edge, build up a wall with the rest of the mixture, about 1 inch higher than the flat part. This is easiest to do if you have a pastry bag and tube (from a kitchen department or a hardware store), but you can also do it by putting small blobs of meringue mix on the circle edge with a teaspoon and smoothing them into a wall with a knife.

Bake for about 1 hour. Test by inserting the point of a small knife into the thickest part to see if it is still moist or sticky inside; if it is, bake for 10 minutes longer. Turn off oven heat, open the door, and allow meringue to dry for an hour.

Filling for Large Pie

1 pint whipping cream
3 tbsp. sugar
½ tsp. vanilla

1 quart strawberries, raspberries, or sliced peaches

Whip the cream stiffly, and flavor with sugar and vanilla. Spread ⅓ of the mixture over the bottom of the pie. On top of this, arrange the fruit; if strawberries are large, they should be cut in half, reserving a few perfect ones for a garnish. Scoop the rest of the cream over to cover the fruit, and decorate with a few perfect berries or peach slices. Keep pie cool until serving time.

8 BAKED BANANAS WITH RUM
SERVES TWO

2 tbsp. butter
2 large firm bananas (slightly green at tip)

3 tbsp. brown sugar
1 tbsp. lemon juice
2 tbsp. rum

Heat oven to 375°. Melt butter in a shallow baking dish. Peel bananas, and cut in half lengthwise. Arrange side by side in the baking dish, and sprinkle over them the sugar, lemon juice, and rum. Bake for 15 minutes, basting once or twice with the liquid in the dish. You can transfer the bananas to a chafing dish if you have one. Heat for a few minutes, then pour over an additional 2 tbsp. rum, set fire to it, and allow to flame for 1 or 2 minutes. The flaming, of course, should be done at the table. Serve two banana halves to each person, spooning sauce over the fruit. If you wish, you may add chopped, unsalted pecans to bananas during baking process.

9 PEACHES MELBA
SERVES FOUR

4 large peach halves, preferably free-stone (canned, or fully ripened fresh ones)

1 pint vanilla ice cream
1 package frozen raspberries

Put the raspberries in the blender, and blend to a purée. Add a little sugar if desired. Put one peach half in each bowl, hollow side up. Fill the hollow with a large scoop of vanilla ice cream, and pour the raspberry purée on top.

10 BAKED PEARS MUMTAZ
SERVES FOUR TO SIX

6 fresh pears, ripe but firm	**6 whole cloves**
1 c. light brown sugar	**A few pieces of candied ginger**
¾ c. water	**1 pint heavy cream**

Wash the pears, and put aside. Preheat oven to 350° for 15 minutes. Meanwhile combine sugar with ¾ c. water in a medium saucepan. Bring to boil, and simmer 5 minutes; remove from heat. Arrange pears in ovenproof baking dish, and stick 1 clove in each. Cut candied ginger into slivers; add to baking dish. Pour sugar syrup over pears, and place on rack in center of oven. Baste pears (with squeeze-bulb baster) every 5 minutes with syrup. Bake 20–30 minutes, or until fruit is tender when pierced with point of knife or toothpick. Do not chill. Serve at room temperature with heavy cream.

11 RICE FOR THE EMPRESS
SERVES FOUR TO SIX

Prepare the day before, to give it time to set.

½ c. rice	**¼ c. cold water**
3 c. cold water	**¼ c. boiling water**
2½ c. hot milk	**¼ c. chopped glacé fruits: citron, orange,**
½ c. sugar	**cherries**
1 tsp. vanilla	**2 tbsp. Cognac or Grand Marnier**
2 egg yolks, beaten	**½ c. whipping cream**
1 envelope gelatin	

Put the rice in a saucepan with the 3 c. cold water. Bring slowly to a full boil, and then drain. Put the drained rice in the top of a double boiler with the hot milk, sugar, and vanilla. Cook over boiling water until very soft and creamy, about 1½ hours, stirring occasionally. Cool slightly, and stir in beaten egg yolks. Soak gelatin in ¼ c. cold water for 5 minutes, then dissolve in the boiling water. Add to rice mixture, and stir well. Chill in refrigerator. Soak the glacé fruit in the Cognac or Grand Marnier. When the rice mixture is beginning to set, stir in the glacé fruit and liqueur, and gently fold in stiffly whipped cream. Pour into a glass or china bowl, and chill for several hours, preferably overnight. Before serving, decorate with a few glacé cherries, or whole strawberries, or toasted slivered almonds. Serve very cold.

12 ENGLISH TRIFLE
SERVES FOUR TO SIX

1 sponge cake, from the bakery or made from a mix
$\frac{1}{2}$ c. raspberry or strawberry jam
$\frac{1}{2}-\frac{3}{4}$ c. medium-sweet sherry
$\frac{1}{4}$ c. slivered almonds
1 package vanilla pudding (instant or cooking type)
2 c. milk
$\frac{1}{2}$ pt. whipping cream
2 tbsp. sugar
$\frac{1}{2}$ tsp. vanilla
Glacé cherries, silver balls, crystallized fruit, for decorating

Split the sponge cake in half to make two layers, and spread one of them liberally with jam. Sandwich with the top half, and put in a crystal or china bowl. Pour sherry evenly over the cake. It should be thoroughly moistened with sherry. Scatter the almonds on top.

Make up the vanilla pudding, cool slightly, then spread over the cake. Chill in the refrigerator. Using a chilled bowl and whisk, whip the cream until stiff, adding sugar and vanilla while beating. Pile the whipped cream on top of the layer of vanilla pudding. Decorate with a pattern of crystallized or glacé fruit and silver balls. If you can't find those, use toasted slivered almonds or walnut halves. Trifle is best when served very cold.

CHAPTER 7

SENSE-REELING DRINKS

The *Bartender's Guide* lists more than thirteen hundred drinks, and new ones are being invented yearly. If you add to this number all the *non*alcoholic beverages, the varieties of wine, and the numerous regional favorites discovered in various corners of the world, it would take an *encyclopedia* even to list them! We're *not* going to be comprehensive; instead, here are a variety of drink ideas to supplement those given with the dinner and brunch menus.

1 TEA

HOT TEA

There are dozens of unique tea flavors, so don't get stuck in the rut of supermarket tea bags. Gourmet shops have loose teas from India, Ceylon, and China; health food shops carry herbal teas such as verbena, mint, camomile, black currant; some firms make special blends of their own. All should be brewed with freshly *boiling* water in a warmed teapot to extract the fullest flavor. Rinse teapot first with boiling water; in a strainer over the pot, place a heaping teaspoon of loose tea for *every two* cups of water. Pour really *boiling* water over tea leaves; let it steep five minutes. Serve with thin slices of lemon, a clove stuck in each.

For a change of pace and flavor, put a few sprigs of mint right *in* the teapot, or two or three cloves, or a piece of cinnamon stick. Or add a shot of rum to a cup of hot tea—very reviving!

ICED TEA

For beautifully clear iced tea put four teaspoons tea into a quart jar, cover with cold water, put on the lid, and "infuse" overnight. Do *not* put in refrigerator. Strain before using; add ice; serves four.

Iced tea may be flavored with lemon juice, a slice of peeled fresh ginger, crushed fresh mint, or a slice of unpeeled orange. Or try it mixed with ginger ale:

2 c. strong, hot tea
$\frac{1}{4}$ c. sugar
Juice of 1 lemon

Mix and chill. Add 1 c. ginger ale and a sprig of mint, and pour over ice.

2 COFFEE

Coffee is a marvelous, varied drink ... if you learn some of the more exotic variations given here. (Note: Ground coffee keeps fresh longer if you store current supply in refrigerator, keep extra on hand in the freezer compartment.

ESPRESSO COFFEE

You should have the proper Italian espresso pot to make this coffee. In the bottom container, put 1 demitasse cup of water for each cup of coffee. Measure 1½–2 tbsp. finely-ground Italian coffee per cup into the coffee basket. Screw on the top container, and set over heat to boil. The water will rise from the bottom con-tainer into the top one. When all the water has risen, your coffee is ready. Remove from heat, and serve immediately with a twist of lemon peel in each demitasse. Or serve with a cinnamon stick as a stirrer, a blob of whipped cream sprinkled with cinnamon or nutmeg, or a tablespoon of rum or brandy in each cup.

TURKISH COFFEE

This must be made in the proper small, long-handled pot with sloping sides. Most Syrian or Armenian groceries have them; the prettiest are of polished brass or copper.

For *each* demitasse cup use:

1 heaping tsp. Turkish coffee (pulverized)
1 tsp. sugar (if you don't like coffee sweet, use ½ tsp.)
1 demitasse cup cold water

Put all ingredients into the pot, and heat over flame. When froth rises, take pot from heat, pour a little of the froth into each cup, tap pot sharply on the stove to settle froth, then heat again. Repeat this process twice more (three times in all), then pour the coffee into cups. It will be quite thick, but most of the grounds quickly settle to the bottom of the cup. You don't *stir* Turkish coffee.

Variation on Turkish coffee, as served in Syria and Lebanon:

When brewing Turkish coffee according to previous recipe, add two or three crushed cardamom seeds to the pot: They provide a delicious aroma. Most Turkish coffee pots are quite small, and the coffee is always brewed in small batches— no more than two or three cups at a time for the best results.

ICED COFFEE

If hot coffee is to be poured over ice, it should be brewed double-strength or the ice will melt and make it too weak and watery.

Alternatively, coffee can be brewed regular strength and chilled in the refrigerator overnight. Or leftover coffee can be made into ice cubes, to avoid diluting iced coffee with watery cubes. You use coffee ice cubes in your *hot* coffee!

A hedonist's delight: Mix strong hot coffee with milk, chill overnight in refrigerator. Serve in a large goblet with giant dollop of sweetened whipped cream.

AFTER-DINNER COFFEE: THREE VARIATIONS

a. Irish Coffee *(serves three)*
1 c. strong hot coffee
4 jiggers Irish whiskey
3 jiggers Cointreau or brandy
¼ c. heavy cream, whipped

Warm whiskey and Cointreau together. Add coffee, and pour into Irish coffee mugs (or small coffee cups). Top with whipped cream.

b. New Orleans Café Brûlot *(serves four)*

Make this in a fondue pot or chafing dish, and flame at the dinner table. In New Orleans a special brûlot bowl is used, rather deeper than a chafing dish. Whichever you use, you will need a small ladle to pour coffee into cups.

4 jiggers brandy
Thinly pared peel of 1 lemon or 1 orange

This is a summer favorite in Hungarian and Viennese cafés.

(or ½ each)
6 cloves
1 piece cinnamon stick
6 lumps sugar
4 demitasse cups extra-strong hot coffee (about 1½ measuring c.)

Put peel, cloves, cinnamon, and sugar into chafing dish (or brûlot bowl if available). Cover with brandy, and warm until sugar is melted. Ignite and allow to flame. While still flaming, pour the hot black coffee into it. Ladle into demitasse cups.

c. Mexican Coffee-Chocolate

Make hot chocolate from an instant chocolate mix, using an equal quantity of strong hot coffee instead of water. Serve with a dollop of whipped cream if desired.

3 MILK, CREAM, YOGURT, IN A VARIETY OF DRINKS

MILK

Milk combines remarkably well with rum, brandy, bourbon, or Scotch, and can be served hot or cold.

a. Cold Milk Punch

Shake with ice 1 or 2 jiggers of any of the above liquors, 1 c. milk, and 1 tbsp. powdered sugar. Strain into a tumbler. Or make with cracked ice in a blender. An

English variation is made without shaking: Pour ¾ c. very cold milk into a glass, add 1 or 2 jiggers preferred liquor and 1 tbsp. sugar, stir well, and fill the glass with well-chilled club soda or ginger ale.

b. Hot Milk Punch *(a comforting and soporific nightcap)*

1 c. hot milk
1–2 jiggers preferred liquor

1½ tbsp. honey
¼ tsp. powdered ginger

Heat honey and ginger with milk

CREAM

Appears as an ingredient in mixed drinks, chiefly in variations of gin fizz, and in Deep South recipes for eggnog.

a. Cream Fizz

To make this, just add to the silver fizz recipe, given under Dinner Menu Number 30, ½–1 tbsp. cream for each serving. This is best made in a blender.

b. Southern-Style Eggnog

This is very rich and should be served in small glasses or cups; quantities given will make about fifteen servings.

6 egg yolks
½ c. sugar
1 c. brandy or bourbon whiskey

YOGURT

This is the basis of some wonderful nonalcoholic drinks, preferably made in a blender. Here are two versions, the first low calorie, and the second a *meal*.

a. Lassi *(a favorite drink in Pakistan)*

½ c. yogurt (plain)
¼ c. water
¼ c. crushed ice (2 or 3 cubes)
1 tbsp. powdered sugar
Vanilla, orange flower water, or rose water to flavor

Put into the blender and whirl until very frothy—delicious served with a hot,

until dissolved. Pour over liquor in a mug or glass, stir, and drink piping hot.

2 c. cream
2 c. milk
3 egg whites
Freshly grated nutmeg

In a large, deep bowl, beat egg yolks until creamy and light-colored. Gradually beat in sugar. Add slowly 1 c. brandy, 1 c. cream, and 2 c. milk. Continue beating as you add all these ingredients. In a separate bowl beat the egg whites until very stiff. In a third bowl beat the remaining 1 c. cream until stiff. Gently fold the egg whites into the whipped cream, then blend them into the first mixture. Grate nutmeg over each serving.

spicy curry.

b. Yogurt-Banana Milk Shake

½ c. plain yogurt
1 small ripe banana
½ c. milk
1 whole egg
2 tbsp. sugar
1 scoop ice cream (optional)

Whirl in the blender until smooth and frothy. This packs enough nourishment to substitute for a meal when it's "just too hot to eat"; you can serve smaller portions as a dessert.

4 FRUIT DRINKS
(with and without alcohol)

Canned fruit juices and frozen concentrates may be combined in many different ways. Experiment and sample . . . add, if desired, vodka, applejack, or one of the fruit-flavored liqueurs, such as Cointreau or Curaçao.

Fresh fruit such as watermelon, honeydew, blueberries, strawberries, raspberries, peaches, ripe plums, mangoes, or papaya may be liquidized with $\frac{1}{2}$ to 1 cup crushed ice in the blender (add sugar if desired) for a delicious drink full of vitamins. This blender special is called *refresco* or *sorbete* in Latin America and is a popular mid-afternoon drink. If the mixture is too thick, it may be diluted with water, club soda, or 7Up. Liquidized watermelon is especially good when mixed with 1 jigger of rum and the juice of half a lime, plus sugar to taste.

COCKTAILS BASED ON FRUIT JUICE

Several of the cocktail recipes given in the dinner menus use lemon, lime, orange, or pineapple juice as an ingredient. Here are two for cranberry juice:

a. Cape Codder

In a highball glass put 3 or 4 ice cubes, add 1 jigger vodka and 4 jiggers cranberry juice. Stir well and serve.

b. Cranberry Fizz

For each drink use 1 jigger gin, 1 jigger cranberry juice, juice of half lemon, and 1–3 tsp. simple syrup. (See recipe for simple syrup under sangria in section 5.) Shake with ice, or mix in a blender with crushed ice. Strain into glasses, and add a splash of club soda.

5 WINE IN MIXED DRINKS

Several suggestions for drinks mixed with wine, vermouth, sherry, etc. are given in the menu chapters. Here are a few more you might like to try:

SPRITZER

Pour chilled white wine to fill a goblet or large wine glass halfway. Add chilled club soda. The juice of a lemon wedge and a twist of lemon gives this drink an extra zip. (You can also make a fine spritzer with *red* wine!)

SANGRIA

There are several different versions of this, all of them well recommended. Try the basic recipe, then the variations, and see which you prefer. It's an excellent drink for a buffet party, as it can be made in a large pitcher or punch bowl, doubling the quantities if necessary.

1 bottle dry red wine (Spanish, Chilean, or Californian)
1 large, thin-skinned orange
2 jiggers Cointreau or brandy
¾ c. club soda
Sugar if desired

Put about a dozen ice cubes into a large pitcher or bowl. Add the red wine and Cointreau or brandy. Wash but do not peel the orange, slice thinly, and add. If desired, sweeten with sugar, or preferably with simple syrup. (Mix 1 c. sugar with 1 c. water, heat until dissolved, boil 5 minutes, and cool. Keep in a jar in the refrigerator, and use as needed for sweetening drinks.) Stir well to mix ingredients, and add about ¾ c. club soda.

Peaches, strawberries, slices of raw apple, or lime may be used instead of, or as well as, the orange slices.

You can also add 1 c. orange juice to the wine, plus ½ c. lemon juice, and omit the soda. Some recipes do not call for the Cointreau or brandy: the sangria can perfectly well be made without them. Serve in good-sized wineglasses.

WHITE WINE CUP

1 bottle dry wine (American, German, or French)
1 jigger brandy
1 jigger Curaçao, Cointreau, or other fruit-flavored liqueur
1 c. club soda or ginger ale
2 slices orange,
2 slices lemon
Sugar or sugar syrup to taste

This is a basic recipe that can be varied in many different ways. Champagne or other sparkling wine may be used and the soda omitted. Fresh fruit, such as sliced peaches or hulled strawberries, may be used instead of orange and lemon. The drink can be made more alcoholic by adding 1 or 2 jiggers of light rum or vodka, less alcoholic by adding orange or pineapple juice. If the wine is very dry, sugar or simple syrup may be added to taste.

Put ice cubes in a pitcher or bowl, add liqueurs and wine, then fruit; stir to mix, and stand in a cool place for ½ to 1 hour. Stir again, sweeten if necessary, and add soda just before serving. If a large punch bowl is used, it is better to use a block of ice rather than cubes; it can be frozen ahead of time in a milk carton, a plastic bowl, or a ring mould.

The quantities given above are enough for six to eight servings; double or triple the recipe for a larger group.

6 BEER, ALE, STOUT, IN MIXED DRINKS

SHANDY GAFF (a favorite pub drink in the British Isles)

In a tall glass or tankard, mix equal parts ale and ginger beer (*not* ginger ale).

BLACK VELVET

In a tall glass or tankard mix equal parts Guinness stout (which is very dark) and chilled champagne. The champagne should be poured in slowly, after the stout, because it makes a heavy froth that will overflow the glass if you try to hurry the process. Traditionally this is served with oysters on the half shell.

7 COLD WEATHER DRINKS

MULLED WINE (serves two to three)

1 c. claret or other red wine
½ c. boiling water
2 or 3 cloves
1 small piece stick cinnamon
1–1½ tbsp. sugar
Thin peel of 1 lemon
Powdered allspice or cinnamon

Put wine, cloves, cinnamon, lemon peel, and sugar into a saucepan. Heat and stir until sugar is melted, but do not boil. Add boiling water, and strain into mugs or into glasses with a silver spoon standing in each (without this precaution, glasses may crack). Sprinkle a pinch of nutmeg or allspice on each serving.

Cider may be substituted for the claret, in which case the addition of 1 jigger rum or brandy is an improvement.

TOM & JERRY (serves six)

This is a sort of hot eggnog, wonderful as a dessert or nightcap on a cold night. Try it at your next ski weekend.

2 eggs
2 tbsp. sugar
⅛ tsp. nutmeg
3 jiggers rum
6 jiggers bourbon
3–4 c. hot milk (or boiling water)

Mix eggs, sugar and nutmeg, and beat (preferably with an electric beater) until pale yellow in color and very thick and creamy. Chill in refrigerator for 1 hour or longer. Set out six pottery or heavy glass mugs. Divide egg mixture equally between the mugs, add ½ jigger rum and 1 jigger bourbon to each, then fill with hot milk or boiling water. Stir, and sprinkle a little more nutmeg on top of each serving.

ATHOLL BROSE (*serves four*)

More like a dessert than a drink, but delicious to top off an elegant dinner.

½ c. heavy cream
¼ c. honey
½ c. Scotch whiskey

Combine cream and honey in a small, heavy saucepan. Heat gently over a low flame until honey is dissolved, stirring all the time. Slowly stir in the whiskey, and heat for a few seconds longer. Serve hot in small demitasse cups or in special Irish coffee glasses.

CHAPTER 8

FINGER FOODS

Having people in for drinks calls for a menu different from one for brunch or dinner. You may ask one or two friends to stop in after work, or give a real cocktail party for twenty or more people. In either case, you need nibble food to accompany the wine or liquor. Two rules: One, it should be possible to eat the nibbles with your fingers, whether you're standing up or perched on the arm of a chair, without any great danger of messy spills on clothes, rugs, or furniture. Two, such food shouldn't need hours of preparation. Too-elaborate canapés may *look* very pretty, but they are a lot of work, and a small kitchen is not the ideal place to make them. Also, most canapé leftovers are absolutely useless; you just *have* to throw them away. (And we don't believe in waste!)

Here are some ideas and recipes for cocktail party food, grouped into four menus with different national accents, all meeting the two preceding requirements. For fewer guests, select just two or three items from one of the menus, or one from each if you prefer.

Keep some of the staples on hand, especially if you adore giving impromptu invitations. We suggest: corn chips, melba toast rounds, miniature sesame crackers, pastry shells, cocktail crackers shaped to hold a filling. Also keep handy a can or two of black and green olives, smoked oysters or clams, tiny imported shrimps, pâté de foie, black or red caviar, anchovy curls or fillets, at least two kinds of cheese, a chunk of hard salami (keep these last two items refrigerated).

TRANSCONTINENTAL CANAPÉ PARTY

serves fifteen to twenty

SUPPLY CHECKLIST

Check supply shelf for the following; if missing any item, add to marketing list:

Sherry or brandy
Oil, vinegar
Mayonnaise
Butter
Salt, cayenne
Tabasco
Curry powder
Garlic
Bay leaf

MARKETING LIST

1 dozen eggs
1 package Roquefort or Danish blue
    cheese (4–6 oz.)
1 8-oz. package cream cheese
½ lb. braunschweiger or liverwurst
1 can crabmeat (6–8 oz.)
3 small cans smoked oysters
2 ripe avocados
2 medium tomatoes, or 1 large, ripe
    but firm
1 lemon
1 bunch each green onions and
    parsley
1 small package shelled pecans or
    walnuts
1 small can truffles or 1 small can
    sliced mushrooms
1 loaf home-style white bread
    (Pepperidge Farm, Arnold, or
    from your local bakery)
½ pint heavy cream
Assorted crackers, cocktail biscuits,
    melba toast rounds

MENU

CALIFORNIA CHEESE-NUT ROLL
CURRIED EGG SPREAD
PARFAIT DE FOIE
GUACAMOLE
NEW ORLEANS DEVILED CRAB
SMOKED OYSTERS

1 PREPARING THE CANAPÉS

CHEESE ROLL

Mash cream cheese and blue cheese, or put through strainer, so that there are no lumps. Beat in 4 tbsp. butter with a fork or electric beater. Add 1 tbsp. finely chopped green onion and 1 tbsp. finely chopped parsley. Season with $\frac{1}{8}$ tsp. cayenne and 3 dashes Tabasco. Add 1–2 tbsp. heavy cream, and refrigerate until cold and firm. Coarsely chop pecans or walnuts, and spread them out on waxed paper or foil. With your hands, press the cheese mixture into a round ball, and roll it in the chopped nuts until well coated on all sides. Refrigerate.

CURRIED EGG

Hard-boil 8 eggs in strongly salted water (use at least 3 tsp.) for 10 minutes. Run cold water over them; shell and chop finely. Melt 2 tbsp. butter in a small skillet, and add 1 tbsp. curry powder. Warm and stir the mixture together. Add to the chopped eggs. Stir in 3 tbsp. mayonnaise, and season with 1 tsp. salt, $\frac{1}{8}$ tsp. cayenne, and Tabasco if desired. Check the seasoning; if you prefer it hotter, add more curry powder, cayenne, or Tabasco. Cover with plastic wrap and refrigerate.

PARFAIT DE FOIE

Chop the truffles or canned mushrooms (should come to 3 tbsp.), and cover with 2 tbsp. brandy or sherry. Mash or sieve the braunschweiger or liverwurst, and stir in 3 tbsp. heavy cream. Season to taste with cayenne and Tabasco, and stir in the chopped truffles with the brandy or sherry they soaked in. Cover and chill.

GUACAMOLE

There are many different versions of this Mexican salad, with or without tomato and moderate or heavy on the garlic. Try ours, then vary it to suit your taste.

Dip the tomatoes into boiling water for a few seconds; chill and skin them. Peel avocados, remove pits, slice and cut into small pieces. Put into a bowl, and add 1 large clove garlic, either put through a garlic press or *very* finely chopped. Add 1 tbsp. oil beaten with $\frac{1}{2}$ tbsp. vinegar and the juice of $\frac{1}{2}$ lemon. Add salt and Tabasco to taste. Cut peeled tomatoes in half, and press out all the juice and seeds. Chop fairly small, and add to avocado. Mash slightly to mix well, preferably with a wooden fork. If you're not serving *at once*, sprinkle *heavily* with lemon juice, cover *tightly* with plastic wrap (both measures to prevent discoloration), and chill.

DEVILED CRAB

Melt 3 tbsp. butter in a skillet; in it, sauté 2 green onions finely chopped, 1 small bay leaf finely crumbled, and 1 clove of garlic minced or crushed. Cut crusts from 3 slices white bread, and dice finely; add to mixture in skillet. Pick through the crabmeat, removing any pieces of shell or membrane. Chop crab finely, and add to skillet. Mash mixture, adding any liquid from crabmeat can. Season with cayenne and black pepper; add salt if necessary. Serve hot.

SMOKED OYSTERS

No preparation necessary except for draining off the oil they're packed in.

2 FINAL ASSEMBLY

Arrange all six appetizers in separate small bowls or on platters; you can place each bowl on a larger plate, and arrange around it a ring of crackers, corn chips, melba toast, and so on, or put all the crackers on one large tray and let people choose their own combinations. The cheese roll and parfait de foie need small knives for spreading; oysters are easiest to spear with a small fork, and the curried egg, deviled crab, and guacamole are probably best scooped up with a teaspoon.

MIDDLE EAST MEZE (may-zay)

serves twelve to sixteen

MENU

cold

STUFFED GRAPE LEAVES
OLIVES, BLACK AND GREEN
WHITE FETA CHEESE
TARAMA SALATA
HUMMUS

hot

FRIED MUSSELS
CHEESE BOREK
POTATO CHEESE PUFFS

SUPPLY CHECKLIST

Check your supply shelf for the following; if missing any item, add to marketing list:

Flour (1¼ c.)
Baking powder
Eggs (3)
Milk
Lemons (3)
Olive oil
Paprika
Salt
Garlic
Butter (1 stick)
Frying fat (2–3 lbs. Crisco, Spry, or other solid shortening—not butter or margarine)

MARKETING LIST

2 large or 4 small cans stuffed grape leaves (30–40 pieces)
2 cans large green olives
¾ lb. Greek (black) olives, in oil
1 lb. feta cheese
2–3 jars tarama salata (fish roe spread)
2 jars hummus (chick pea dip)

All the above may be bought in cans or jars from a Greek, Armenian, Syrian, or Lebanese delicatessen, or from the gourmet section of a large supermarket or department store.

1½ quarts fresh mussels or 3 cans mussels (40–50 pieces)
1 package filo pastry, from a Greek delicatessen or frozen from a supermarket
1 large container small-curd cottage cheese
1 can grated Parmesan cheese
3 packages frozen potato puffs
1 bunch parsley
1 bunch fresh dill, if obtainable

1 PRELIMINARIES

The first five items on marketing list are practically ready to serve. Grape leaves, olives, cheese, and tarama salata need only to be refrigerated until guests arrive.

The hummus may need a little extra seasoning—taste it, and if it seems bland, add 1–2 cloves crushed garlic, juice of $\frac{1}{2}$ lemon, 1–2 tbsp olive oil, and a little salt. It should be served in a bowl; with the back of a spoon, make a depression in the middle of the hummus, into which you pour 1 tbsp. olive oil mixed with 1 tsp. paprika. Garnish with a sprig of parsley.

If you use fresh mussels, precook them the day before the party as follows: Preheat oven to 450°. Wash the mussels in their shells very thoroughly several times, and scrub with a stiff brush. Discard any open shells. Spread out on a large baking pan, and put into oven until the shells open (7–10 minutes). Remove from oven, and throw away any shells still closed. Take mussels out of shells, trim off any shaggy black edges, and refrigerate overnight. (Save pan juice to add to chowder or another fish dish later—it's delicious!)

2 PREPARING THE APPETIZERS

On the day of the party, prepare the three hot dishes as follows:

CHEESE BOREK

INGREDIENTS:
6 sheets filo pastry
1 stick butter, melted
2 eggs
1 large container cottage cheese
2 tbsp. finely chopped parsley
2 tbsp. finely chopped fresh dill, if obtainable

METHOD:

Preheat oven to 350°. Grease two 8-inch-square baking pans or two 9-inch round pie tins. Divide in half each of 6 sheets of filo pastry. Lay one piece in each tin, and brush with butter; then lay a second and third on top of the first, brushing each layer with butter. (Let the dough overlap the tin at the sides; this will be folded over at the end.)

Beat 2 eggs and mix with cottage cheese; add chopped parsley and dill. Spread half the mixture evenly on top of the pastry in each baking tin. On top of the cheese mixture, place another sheet of

POTATO CHEESE PUFFS

Spread puffs out on a large baking sheet, and heat in oven according to package directions. When *half*-cooked, remove from oven, and brush with 4 tbsp. melted

FRIED MUSSELS

INGREDIENTS:
Mussels (cooked or canned)
1½ c. flour
1 tsp. baking powder
1¼ tsp. salt
1 egg
1¼ c. milk
1 3-lb. can frying fat (Crisco, Spry, or other solid shortening)

METHOD:
Heat fat over a very low flame in a deep heavy pan. Start with about ⅔ of the shortening, and add more as you need. Prepare fritter batter by sifting flour, baking powder, and salt together; then beat in egg and milk. Beat with an electric or rotary beater until smooth. Dip mussels into batter (it is easiest to spear them on a long-handled fork), drain for a few seconds, and drop them into hot, deep fat. The fat should

pastry; brush with butter, and repeat the process until all pastry is used. Fold the overlap sections over the contents of the tins toward the middle, and brush again with the remaining butter. Bake until crisp and golden (about 25–30 minutes). Cut into individual portions with a sharp knife, and serve hot.

butter mixed with 4 tbsp. grated Parmesan cheese. Return to oven to finish cooking and browning. Serve hot.

be at a temperature of 375°. If you don't have a fat thermometer, check the heat with a cube of bread. It should bob up to the surface and start to turn golden brown in less than 1 minute. Mussels will take about 1½–2 minutes to cook golden brown and crisp. Skim them out, and drain on paper towels.

Serve hot, and sprinkle each with a little paprika.

3 FINAL ASSEMBLY

Cut feta cheese into small cubes, and spear with toothpicks. Also stick toothpicks into stuffed grape leaves, and garnish with small sections of lemon. Serve tarama salata and hummus in bowls, surrounded by crackers or melba toast to spread on. Put green and black olives in bowls. Spear fried mussels and potato puffs with toothpicks, and serve on a warmed plate. Small slices of cheese borek, very hot, are to be eaten with the fingers, but be sure to provide plenty of paper cocktail napkins.

In Turkey these goodies are eaten as an accompaniment to raki or ouzo (Turkish or Greek liqueur) on the rocks, while listening to Turkish folk songs or watching a belly dancer! If raki or ouzo are not available, gin or vodka martinis are fine.

DANISH SMØRREBRØD *(miniature open-faced sandwiches)*

serves eight to ten

Oskar Davidsen's is a world-famous restaurant in Copenhagen which specializes in open-faced sandwiches; the menu, about two feet long, lists nearly two hundred possible combinations. Each is a work of art, a precisely composed still life. You can use the technique, and some of the original ideas, as the basis for cocktail party food in the U.S.

SUPPLY CHECKLIST

Check supply shelf for the following; if missing any item, add to marketing list:

Salt, pepper
Paprika
Bottled capers
Toothpicks

MARKETING LIST

½ lb. rare roast beef, sliced *thin,* from delicatessen
2 cans small shrimps, imported if available
2 small or 1 large jar herring fillets in cream sauce
¼ lb. smoked salmon, Nova Scotia or Scotch
1 large or 2 small cans pâté de foie (6–8 oz. all together)
1 8-oz. stick or package smoked cheese
1 bunch watercress
1 lb. small firm ripe tomatoes or cherry tomatoes
1 lb. medium-size red onions
2 small cucumbers
1 bunch parsley
½ dozen eggs
2 cans sliced pimento
1 jar marinated whole mushrooms
1 small can anchovy curls
1 jar sweet pickled midget gherkins
4 packages German-style pumpernickel or 2–3 loaves dark, firm pumpernickel-style bread
1 carton whipped sweet butter
1 jar capers (optional)

MENU

COLD RARE ROAST BEEF AND RED ONION SLICE
TINY SHRIMP AND CUCUMBER
HERRING IN CREAM SAUCE WITH PIMENTO SLICE
SMOKED SALMON AND COLD SCRAMBLED EGG
LIVER PÂTÉ WITH PICKLED MUSHROOM AND ANCHOVY FILLET
SMOKED CHEESE WITH TOMATO SLICE AND GHERKIN

1 PRELIMINARIES

Make one kind of sandwich at a time. As each variety is finished, set on a plate or baking sheet and cover with plastic wrap. Keep as many as possible in the refrigerator; bread will dry in the open air. (In an emergency, moist paper towels to cover will keep them moist.)

Divide pumpernickel slices in half, making 2 oblong pieces about 4 inches by $2\frac{1}{2}$ inches. Cut off crusts and trim into even-sized oblongs.

2 PREPARING THE APPETIZERS

ROAST BEEF, RED ONION, AND WATERCRESS

Spread 8 pumpernickel slices with whipped butter. Arrange roast beef slices evenly on bread. With a very sharp knife, trim off any edges that hang over, and tuck the pieces under the top layer of beef. Arrange 2 rings of red onion overlapping each other on top of the beef, and where the rings intersect, tuck in a tiny sprig of watercress.

SHRIMP AND CUCUMBER

Spread 8 pumpernickel slices with whipped butter, being sure you cover bread to edge. Down the middle, arrange a row of shrimps closely lined up side by side. Press them down a little so they adhere to butter. Choose fairly small, thin cucumbers for this; if they are too fat, the slices will cover the shrimps instead of serving as a border. Run tines of a fork down the length of the cucumbers, then slice thin. Divide each slice in half, and arrange around the shrimps, keeping the straight edge of the cucumber lined up with the edge of the bread, and pressing it down on the butter so it sticks. The cucumber semicircles should look like a frame. Sprinkle with a little paprika.

HERRING IN CREAM SAUCE WITH PIMENTO

Spread 8 pumpernickel slices with butter. Drain excess cream from herring fillets; split in two any thick or chunky pieces, and flatten them with the side of the knife. Spread evenly over the buttered bread. Sprinkle lightly with chopped parsley, and arrange strips of pimento crosswise like the rungs of a ladder, 4 strips to each slice.

SMOKED SALMON WITH COLD SCRAMBLED EGG

Beat 4 eggs lightly with $\frac{1}{2}$ tsp. salt and $\frac{1}{4}$ tsp. black pepper. Melt 2 tbsp. butter in a skillet and scramble eggs very lightly, leaving them still soft and creamy; they get firmer as they cool.

Spread 8 pumpernickel slices with butter, and add cooled scrambled egg on top. Add 2 or 3 narrow strips of smoked salmon to form a cross, allowing the egg to show at the sides. Put a caper in the middle, and spear with a toothpick.

LIVER PÂTÉ WITH MUSHROOM AND ANCHOVY

Spread 8 pumpernickel slices with butter. Arrange 8 slices of well-chilled liver pâté on them. Make a small indentation in the middle of each slice, and arrange in it a small marinated mushroom, hollow side up. In each hollow put an anchovy curl, and spear it with a toothpick.

SMOKED CHEESE WITH TOMATO AND GHERKIN

Spread 8 pumpernickel slices with butter. Cut smoked cheese into 16 slices or rings. Put 2 pieces on each slice of bread, and press down to be sure they stick to butter. On each, arrange a slice of tomato (or 2 halves if using cherry tomatoes). Slash 8 gherkins lengthwise 3–4 times but *not* all the way through; spread slices out like a fan. Arrange over tomato, and anchor with a toothpick.

3 FINAL ASSEMBLY

At serving time, arrange a selection of each variety of sandwich on a large platter.

The best drink to serve is icy cold Tuborg or Carlsberg lager beer; or Danish akvavit in a shot glass, with the lager beer as a chaser (optional.) Akvavit is powerful, so keep glasses small!

ENGLISH PUB PARTY
serves nine to twelve

SUPPLY CHECKLIST
Check your supply shelf for the following; if missing any item, add to marketing list:

Butter ($\frac{1}{2}$ lb.)
Bread crumbs
Nutmeg
Cayenne
Worcestershire sauce
Flour
Toothpicks
Frying fat (2–3 lbs. Crisco, Spry, or other solid shortening—not butter or margarine)

MARKETING LIST
1 dozen eggs, smallest size
$1\frac{1}{2}$ lbs. sausage meat or link sausage
1 lb. aged Cheddar cheese
1 box melba toast or small plain crackers
1 box wheatmeal biscuits or Pilot crackers
2 cans kipper snacks
3 cans tiny imported shrimps
2 cans oysters
1 lb. thinly sliced bacon
1 package piecrust mix
1 jar grated Parmesan cheese
$\frac{1}{2}$ bottle port wine (red) or medium sherry

MENU
SCOTCH EGGS
POTTED SHRIMPS
WINE MERCHANTS' CHEESE
KIPPER SNACKS
CHEESE STRAWS
ANGELS ON HORSEBACK

1 PREPARING THE CANAPES

SCOTCH EGGS

Detailed instructions on preparation of Scotch eggs are given under Brunch Menu Number 8. For a cocktail snack, omit the mustard sauce and use smallest size eggs. You can hard-boil and shell the eggs, wrap them in sausage meat, and dip them in egg and bread crumbs ahead of time, even the night before the party, but fry them shortly before serving, so that they are hot, fresh, and crisp on the outside when served.

POTTED SHRIMPS

Melt $\frac{1}{2}$ stick (2 oz.) butter in a skillet; drain shrimps, and warm them gently in the butter. Add $\frac{1}{8}$ tsp. cayenne and $\frac{1}{8}$ tsp. grated nutmeg, or more to taste. Put into a bowl or crock, and when cool, pour over an additional 2 tbsp. of melted butter. Refrigerate for several hours. Serve in the bowl, surrounded by crackers or melba toast.

WINE MERCHANTS' CHEESE

Trim off rind of Cheddar cheese, and put cheese through a meat grinder or food mill. If you don't have either of these, mash the cheese a little at a time with a fork on a chopping board. Pound or mash into the cheese $\frac{1}{4}$ lb. butter, a good pinch of cayenne, and a dash of Worcestershire sauce. Add $\frac{1}{4}$ c. port wine or sherry, or more to taste. Mix well together, and put in a deep crock. This is best if made several days ahead of time, so the flavor blends well. Take out of refrigerator 1 hour before the party. Serve with English wheatmeal biscuits or Pilot crackers.

KIPPER SNACKS

No preparation necessary. Serve as is, speared with toothpicks, or surrounded by small crackers, melba toast rounds, or slices of long rye bread to spread them on.

CHEESE STRAWS

Prepare piecrust mix according to package directions, and roll out into a rectangular shape. Brush all over with melted butter ($\frac{1}{8}$ lb.), and sprinkle thickly with grated Parmesan cheese. Fold $\frac{1}{3}$ of the pastry toward the middle, lap the opposite side over it, and roll out again to about $\frac{1}{2}$-inch thickness. Cut into narrow strips $\frac{1}{2}$ inch wide and 3–4 inches long. Beat 1 egg (you should have 1 left over after making the Scotch eggs), mix with any remains of the melted butter, and brush over the top of the strips. Sprinkle lightly with additional Parmesan, and bake according to package directions until golden brown and crisp. Cheese straws can be made ahead of time and stored in a tin; but if so, warm in 350° oven for a few minutes before serving.

ANGELS ON HORSEBACK

Drain oysters, and pat dry with paper towels. Cut bacon strips in half, and wrap each oyster in a piece of bacon. Fix firmly in position with toothpicks, or thread on skewers. Arrange on a broiling rack placed in a large baking tin, and bake in a 400° oven until bacon is crisp and lightly browned, 5–7 minutes. Drain on paper towels, and serve piping hot, speared with toothpicks. (If you cooked them on toothpicks, take these out and replace them with fresh clean ones.)

2 FINAL ASSEMBLY

This assortment of food will happily accompany almost any choice of drinks from beer to Scotch or martinis. It is fairly hearty eating, and could easily keep you from starvation until after a double feature.

AFTERWORD
HOW-TO-COOK-BY-THE-BOOK

Heavens! As Editor-in-Chief of Cosmopolitan Books, I read or scan over forty books a month, and it seems *everybody* (*and* his kissin' cousin) has written a cookbook . . . approximately two thousand in print and about two hundred more published every year!

You might think it's *easy* to write such a book—it *isn't!* As cookbook author and critic Nika Hazelton puts it: "There is just so much food and just so many ways of cooking it." True. However, I've decided the *best* books are written by people who truly savor culinary pleasures, understand how to communicate knowledge, exhibit both imagination and *gusto*.

So, how *do* you tell a "good" cookbook from a "poor" one? *That* isn't easy either—short of buying the book and testing at least half-a-dozen recipes (one method to a speedy bankruptcy!)

First of all, there are so many *kinds* of cookbooks—ones with basic information and *general* recipes, ethnic collections, regional specialties,

single-subject volumes. What expert opinion can you consult and really *rely* on?

The truth is that cookbooks are highly *personal* . . . and although several experts' lists of "the best" *might* include identical choices in some instances, everyone would have *his* own favorite.

Cosmo Cookery was planned as both a kitchen primer and menu sampler. We fervently hope (and believe!) you'll have only *happy* results from our suggestions, will *love* being called a terrific cook, and will want to add to your cookbook shelf for more great meals to come. Where to start?

Before buying a cookbook, simply browse in the cookbook section of your largest bookstore . . . see what especially tempts *you* . . . read a sample recipe to see if it is clear and easy to follow . . . read the foreword or introduction to determine whether the author's feelings about food are interesting.

I've collected books on food from around the world for fifteen years . . . looked at hundreds, cooked from dozens, and my list of favorites follows:

PRIMERS & BASIC GENERAL COOKBOOKS

1. KITCHEN PRIMER, Craig Claiborne (Alfred A. Knopf, Inc., 1969, $6.95).

   For many years Mr. Claiborne was the highly respected food editor of *The New York Times*. He loves food, is an excellent cook, and knows how to explain basics. Line drawings illustrate techniques and equipment. Recipes concentrate on fundamentals of good cooking, are simple to prepare and yield tasty results.

2. THE JAMES BEARD COOKBOOK (E. P. Dutton & Company, Inc., revised 1969, $6.95).

   Mr. Beard enjoys cooking and *especially* eating. I've never seen a picture of him preparing a meal when he didn't sport a grin. The word gusto was *invented* for James Beard, I'm sure. This is an excellent basic cookbook . . . from the "Don't" chapter through an entire cooking repertoire. I've never made a Beard recipe that failed. His taste is hearty and man-oriented. Especially recommended is the paperback version of this book (Dell, $1.25) . . . my choice for the *one* cookbook I wouldn't leave behind.

3. THE JOY OF COOKING, Irma S. Rombauer and Marion Rombauer Becker (The Bobbs-Merrill Co., Inc., revised 1963, $6.95; deluxe edition, $10.00).

   This is absolutely the best information-packed basic cookbook published in America. But, alas, it's got *so much* in it that the publisher has used small type and thin pages to jam it all in . . . from diagrams of all cuts of meat to information on home freezing, nutritional rules, sample menus, and on and on. I can't imagine *anything* that's left out. It belongs on any earnest cook's book shelf . . . and should be consulted on everything, even if you use a variation of a recipe taken from another book. You can trust the information implicitly. And if you're lucky enough to ever track down the edition published in the thirties, you'll be rewarded with all the marvelous food anecdotes Mrs. Rombauer included then, most of which, regrettably, have been eliminated from recent editions.

ETHNIC COOKBOOKS

1. FRENCH

MASTERING THE ART OF FRENCH COOKING, Simone Beck, Louisette Bertholle, and Julia Child, Volume I (Alfred A. Knopf, Inc., 1961, $10.00); Volume II (1970, $12.50).

Yes, this is the famous cookbook by TV's French Chef. It's excellent *if* you have hours to devote to the preparation of a classic French meal, and the patience to do *exactly* what Mrs. Child says. (*No* cookbook author explains herself quite as precisely as Julia Child, so you *can't* go wrong!) The results are superior . . . and some of the recipes unsurpassed, in my opinion, in any other French cookbook available in America. (Note especially the soufflé and quiche recipes—both marvelous for brunches.)

LUCHOW'S GERMAN COOKBOOK, Jan Mitchell (Doubleday & Company, Inc., 1952, $3.50).

As the owner of Lüchow's, a famous New York City restaurant that serves German food, beers, and wines, Mr. Mitchell did all cooks a wonderful service by writing down the recipes prepared by Lüchow's master cooks since the restaurant's founding in 1882. Dishes range from mistake-proof to difficult *haute cuisine,* and are mostly hearty fare that men *adore.* I've *never* known a man to turn down third helpings of simple boiled beef with horseradish sauce. Recipes for sauerbraten, Wiener schnitzel, potato salad, and easy-but-voluptuous German dessert pancakes are *definitive.* Marvelous party idea: a May-wine festival (the traditional recipe is here —add herbs, champagne, and other delights to Moselle or Rhine wine) to intrigue brunch guests . . . in May, *natürlich!*

3. CHINESE
THE PLEASURES OF CHINESE COOKING, Grace Zia Chu (Simon and Schuster, 1962, $4.95; paperback, Cornerstone Library, $1.00).
Madame Chu is a gifted cook and has taught many the delights of her native cuisine. The book is charming to read, easy to cook by. She explains what Chinese food is, utensils needed, how to chop (essential), and delectable recipes to try. It's as complete as cooking lessons!

4. INDIAN
Now that the proper ingredients for cooking exotic foods are available nearly everywhere, there is a surge of interest in the foods of India. The best book:
A TASTE OF INDIA, Mary S. Atwood (Houghton Mifflin Company, 1969, $6.00).
Again, a cooking course between two covers: You'll learn what special Indian ingredients are, how they are combined, the way to serve an Indian meal. Recipes are accurate, imaginative, and the results bring *ahs* of praise from guests. Princess Mumtaz had a lot going for her, and food wasn't the *least* of it!

5. ARMENIAN
TREASURED ARMENIAN RECIPES (Armenian General Benevolent Union, Inc., 109 East 40 Street, New York, N. Y., 1949, $4.00 plus $.25 for shipping).
A bit of ancestral pride goes into this choice. My mother is a simply marvelous Armenian cook who educated her children's palate to subtle flavors never forgotten. Among the specialties: the finest rice recipe *anywhere* (unless you prefer mushy-gush!); delicious spinach omelette, Katah (a marvelous coffee bread), stuffed grapeleaves and mussels, an entire chapter on eggplants. Not for everyone . . . but if you're intrigued, you won't regret it.

6. ITALIAN
ITALIAN FOOD, Elizabeth David (Alfred A. Knopf, Inc., 1958, $6.00).
Mrs. David is one of England's leading food authorities, and clearly enjoys Italian cuisine. She describes markets, fishing centers, regional specialties, wines, in addition to classic Italian foods. The recipes are simply written and first class. Nothing in this book swims in tomato sauce, bless her!

7. MEXICAN
ELENA'S SECRETS OF MEXICAN COOKING, Elena Zelayeta (Prentice-Hall, Inc., 1958, $5.95).
This book is a *double* inspiration: Not only do the recipes make the best Mexican food I've ever eaten, but the remarkable and famous cook is blind! Elena's joy in life adds something special to her recipes—from guacamole (aah!) to a Tequila sour (ooh!)

8. MIDDLE EASTERN
MIDDLE EASTERN COOKING (Time-Life Books, 1969, $7.95).
Classic recipes from the nine Middle Eastern

nations: Greece, Turkey, Syria, Lebanon, Israel, Jordan, Egypt, Iraq, Iran. Lamb is the basic meat, but the varieties of appetizers, soups, vegetables, salads, and desserts are endless . . . from the plain to the exotic. Magnificent pictures and a good deal of informative material in addition to the recipes. (The Lebanese tabbouleh salad is the biggest hit at all my summer parties!

9. RUSSIAN

RUSSIAN COOKING (Time-Life Books, 1969, $7.95).

The five major cuisines of the fifteen Soviet republics are explored in considerable detail. Again, the background information and the photographs are fascinating . . . the recipes succulent. You can learn all about caviar, *at last,* and proceed to chicken Kiev and other Russian delights.

SPECIALIZED COOKBOOKS

1. THE BLENDER COOKBOOK, Ann Seranne and Eileen Gaden (Doubleday & Company, Inc., 1961, $5.50).

Excellent recipes from drinks to sauces to desserts. If you have a blender, treat yourself!

2. VEGETARIAN GOURMET COOKERY, Alan Hooker (101 Productions, 1970, $3.95).

If you're into vegetarian food, you'll find Mr. Hooker's ideas very tasty indeed: high-protein entrées, breads, desserts . . . all are here along with herb blends, sauces, cooking tips. Paperback, with nice line drawings, easy-to-read recipes.

3. THE ART OF FINE BAKING, Paula Peck (Simon and Schuster, 1970, $6.50; paperback, $2.95).

Ah, the smell of something baking . . . and this lady is an *expert!* Baking *anything* terrified me until Mrs. Peck came to the rescue. Her directions are clear (supplemented by baby-simple illustrations when necessary), the results excellent. Yes, you can buy delicious frozen and bakery products . . . *but,* bake something yourself for the man/men in your life, and see your super-person rating rise, right with the dough!

4. THE COMPLETE BOOK OF HOME BAKING, Ann Seranne (Doubleday & Company, Inc., 1950, $6.95).

This is a baking bible, filled with every variety of pastry goodie, including apple pandowdy! You won't know what to try first!

MISCELLANEOUS

1. THE NEW YORK TIMES LARGE TYPE COOKBOOK, Jean Hewitt (Golden Press, 1968, $9.95).

The book is large, the type huge and so easy to read without burrowing into the pages. The recipes are a potpourri . . . selected by Miss Hewitt, home economist of *The New York Times,* whom I consider practically infallible. The Hungarian paprika goulash is ideal for a hot buffet for six!

2. BEETON'S BOOK OF HOUSEHOLD MANAGEMENT, A first edition facsimile (Farrar, Straus & Giroux, Inc., 1969, $12.95.)

The remarkable Mrs. Isabella Beeton was a Victorian lady who wrote this book in 1861. Her husband's firm published it and was saved from bankruptcy by its success. More than one thousand pages cover The Mistress (no, not *that* one!), General Observation of Quadrupeds, Invalid Cookery, Domestic Servants, The Rearing and Management of Children, Diseases of Infancy and Childhood, The Doctor, Legal Memoranda. A classic of domestic literature, lots of fun to read, and a very special gift for anyone *really* interested in food and its history. I adore it!

One last word: there is no mystique about talent for cooking. It takes time, and desire. Repeat your successes, forget the failures. Save the best of your recipes, and file them away carefully. *Use* your books. I write the date next to any recipe I try, and my opinion. Or if I've made additions to a recipe, I write them in . . . next time no *guess*work.

And *do* enjoy yourself!

Jeanette Sarkisian Wagner
EDITOR-IN-CHIEF
COSMOPOLITAN BOOK CLUB

INDEX

Abbreviations, vii
Almonds, deviled, 35
Americano cocktail, 92–93
Angels on Horseback, 236
Antipasto, 92, 134, 160
Apple cake, 203–204
Appliances, 4, 7
Atholl Brose, 219

B

Bacardi cocktail, 83
Baking dishes, 5, 7
Baltic cocktail, 39
Bananas, baked, with rum, 207
Bananas, Crunchy, 126
Basque Tortilla Diablo, 177
Beef
  in aspic, 149
  Granatine, 62–63
  roulades, 62–63
Beets and green beans vinaigrette, 71
Black Velvet, 218
Blanquette de veau, 146
Bloody Mary, 175, 195
Blueberry rum tarts, 202
Brandy sour, 99
Brunches
  for four, 166–168, 169–171, 172–173, 174–175, 176–178, 184–186, 187–189, 196–198
  for six, 179–181
  for two, 182–183, 190–192, 193–195
Bullshot cocktail, 173

C

Casserole dishes, 5, 7
Cheese Borek, 228–229
Cheese croutons, 59
Cheese roll, 225
Cheese straws, 235
Cheese, Toasted Tidbits, 68
Cheese, Wine Merchant's, 235
Chef's Salad, Gypsy's, 180
Chicken
  French, 140
  Guillermo, 152
  Korean, 95
  Legs Fair and Fowl, 119
  Luau, 68
  Marili, 107
  Paella, 137
  Veronica, 86
Chicken livers vin rouge, 33
China, 21–22
Chocolate mousse, French, 203
Coffee, 212–214
Cookbooks, 238–241
Coquilles de fruits de mer, 197–198
Crab, deviled, 226
Crackers, deviled, 53
Cranberry fizz, 216
Cream drinks, 215
Crêpes de volaille gratinées, 191–192
Crudités, 47
Cucumber-caviar appetizer, 65
Cucumber Raita, 143–144

D

Daiquiri, 87, 155
  strawberry, 178
Danish smørrebrød, 231–233
Dinners
  cook-ahead, 136–161
  for four, 34–36, 55–57, 64–66, 76–78, 79–81, 103–105, 106–108, 130–132, 133–135, 136–138, 142–144, 145–147, 148–150, 151–152, 153–155, 156–158
  for four to six, 159–161
  for six to eight, 127–129
  for two, 26–28, 29–31, 32–33, 37–39, 40–42, 43–45, 46–48, 49–51, 52–54, 58–60, 61–63, 67–69, 70–72, 73–75, 82–84, 85–87, 88–90, 91–93, 94–96, 97–99, 100–102, 109–111, 112–114, 115–117, 118–120, 121–123, 124–126, 139–141
Dressings, salad
  French, 59, 74, 77
  ravigote, 41
  vinaigrette, 71

E

Eggnog, 215
Eggs
  curried, 225
  Farmer's Breakfast, 194–195
  Florentine, 175
  foo yong, 173
  hardboiled, 89
  Russian, 30
  Scotch, 185–186, 235
Espresso, 213

F

Farmer's Breakfast, 194–195
Filet mignon Charleville, 131
Fillet of sole Florentine, 44–45
Fish
  coquilles de fruits de mer, 197–198
  kedgeree, 188
  Malayan, 77
  salade Niçoise, 59
  salmon steak, cold poached, 154
  sole, fillet of, Florentine, 44–45

Fondue, Swiss cheese, 56
French dressing, 59, 74, 77
Fruit drinks, 216

G

Gimlet, 188
Gin and tonic, 59–60, 90
Gingerbread Imperial, 204
Glassware, 21–22
Grapefruit, honey-broiled, 128
Guacamole, 225
Gypsy's Chef's Salad, 180

H

Ham
  slice flambé, 35–36
  steak New Orleans, 50
Hangtown Fry, 183

J

Jack Rose cocktail, 158

K

Kedgeree, 188
Kidneys Vert Pré, 113
Kir cocktail, 75
Kirsch-Dubonnet cocktail, 57

L

Lamb
  curry, 143
  Espagnol, 65
  Lambalaya, 125
  shish kebab, 116
  steaks, savory, 83
Lassi, 215
Lighting, 4
Linens, 19–21
Lobster
  fra diavolo, 30
  Lovable, 122
  tails, broiled, 74

M

Manhattan cocktail, 63, 101, 147
Margarita cocktail, 138
Martini, dry, 48, 150
Meatball and eggplant casserole, 160
Meringues, 205–207
Milk drinks, 214–215
Mousse, French chocolate, 203
Mulled wine, 218
Mulligatawny soup, 53
Mushrooms à la Grecque, 50
Mussels, fried, 229

O

Old-fashioned cocktail, 152
Osso buco, 80
Oysters
    Angels on Horseback, 236
    Hangtown Fry, 183
    smoked, 119, 226

P

Paella, 137
Parfait de Foie, 225
Peaches Melba, 207
Pears, baked, Mumtaz, 208
Pears in wine syrup, 107
Pineapple-rum cocktail, 69
Pork chops
    Borracho, 157
    New Orleans, 47–48
    Senegalese, 38
Potato-cheese puffs, 229
Potatoes
    baked, 62
    buttered new, 86
    Chantilly, 122
    mashed, ramekins of, 113
    rissolées, 44
Pots and pans, 5, 7
Pound Cake en Surprise, 204–205

Q

Quiche Lorraine, 167

R

Rajah's peg, 192
Ravigote dressing, 41
Relish platter, 62
Rice
    for the Empress, 208–209
    green, 27, 28
    pilaf, 33
Rob Roy cocktail, 45, 126, 161
Rock Cornish game hens, sherried, 41–42

S

Salad
    avocado, 107
    avocado-grapefruit, 119
    avocado-tomato, 44
    cucumber, wilted, 154–155
    endive, 33
    endive and watercress, 128–129
    green, 64–65, 79–80, 96, 116, 124–125, 136–137,
        156–157
    green, mixed, 46–47, 103, 112–113, 151–152
    green, tossed, 34–35, 130–131
    Gypsy's Chef, 180
    Mimosa, 149–150
    Niçoise, 59
    orange-avocado, 53, 68
    orange-onion, 38, 144
    spinach and watercress, 147
    tomato, 98, 110, 122, 140, 183
Salade Niçoise, 59
Salami and prosciutto roulades, 56
Salmon steak, cold poached, 154
Salty Dog, 180
Sangria, 217
Scampi Guadalajara, 110
Scotch eggs, 185–186, 235
Screwdriver, 183
Senegalese soup, 89
Shandy Gaff, 218
Sherry cocktail, 42
    and bitters, 78
    Reform Club, 51
Shish kebab, 116
Shrimp

Avocado Louise, 89
Polynesian, 53–54
potted, 95, 235
Scampi Guadalajara, 110
Springtime, 27
Sidecar cocktail, 132
Silver, 21
Silver Fizz, 114, 167
Sirloin Surprise, 101
Smoked Oysters Supreme, 119
Smørrebrød, 231–233
Spaghetti carbonara, 104
Spedini alla Romana, 170
Spritzer, 216
Staple foods, 11–15
Steak au poivre, 98
Storage space, 3–4, 7
Strawberry Valentine soufflé, 202–203
Supplies, kitchen, 3–15
Swiss cheese fondue, 56

T

Table settings, 19–23
Tarts, blueberry rum, 202
Tea, 212
Tom and Jerry, 218
Tomato juice, spiced, 170
Tomatoes, broiled, 175
Tomatoes, cold stuffed, 131
Trifle, English, 209

Turkey Tetrazzini, 128
Turkish coffee, 213

U

Utensils, 5–6, 7–8

V

Valentine Dinner, 121–123
Veal
blanquette de veau, 146
chops Milano, 92
osso buco, 80
scaloppine Marsala, 134
Vermouth, 28
sweet, 81, 104, 135
Vinaigrette sauce, 71
Vodka, 66, 120
Baltic cocktail, 39
Gibson, 144
Martini, 31, 108

W

Whiskey Mac, 186
Whiskey Sour, 54, 111, 140–141
White wine cup, 217

Y

Yams, baked, 50
Yogurt drinks, 215
Yogurt relish, 62

The text of this book is set in 10 point Optima with 3
points leading. The headings, menus, and cooking
directions are in larger sizes of Optima and Optima
Bold. The Optima face is the work of Herman Zapf,
noted type designer born in Nürnberg, Germany, in
1918. Zapf has also designed Melior, Palatino, and
many other types widely used in contemporary
bookmaking.
The art nouveau face used for the book and chapter
titles is Benguiat Laurent, an original hand-lettered
design by Edward Benguiat for Photo-Lettering, Inc.

Book design and covers by Dorris Crandall
Composed by Book Graphics, Inc.